SWORD
BEACH

The 'Battle Zone Normandy' Series

Orne Bridgehead Lloyd Clark
Sword Beach Ken Ford
Juno Beach Ken Ford
Gold Beach Simon Trew
Omaha Beach Tim Bean
Utah Beach Stephen Badsey
Villers-Bocage George Forty
Battle for Cherbourg Robin Havers
Operation Epsom Lloyd Clark
Battle for St-Lô Nigel de Lee
Battle for Caen Simon Trew
Operation Cobra Christopher Pugsley
Road to Falaise Steve Hart
Falaise Pocket Paul Latawski

All of these titles can be ordered via the
Sutton Publishing website
www.suttonpublishing.co.uk

The 'Battle Zone Normandy'
Editorial and Design Team
Series Editor Simon Trew
Senior Commissioning Editor Jonathan Falconer
Assistant Editor Nick Reynolds
Cover and Page Design Martin Latham
Editing and Layout Donald Sommerville
Mapping Map Creation Ltd
Photograph Scanning and Mapping Bow Watkinson
Index Michael Forder

SWORD BEACH

KEN FORD

Series Editor: Simon Trew

Foreword:
Maj-Gen J.C.B. Sutherell

Sutton Publishing

First Published in 2004 by
Sutton Publishing Limited · Phoenix Mill
Thrupp · Stroud · Gloucestershire · GL5 2BU

Text Copyright © Ken Ford 2004
Tour map overlays Copyright © Sutton
    Publishing
Tour base maps Copyright © Institut
    Géographique National, Paris
GSGS (1944) map overlays Copyright ©
    Sutton Publishing
GSGS (1944) base maps Copyright ©
    The British Library/Crown Copyright

Ken Ford has asserted the moral right to be
identified as the author of this work.

British Library Cataloguing in Publication Data
A catalogue record for this book is available
from The British Library.

ISBN 0-7509-3019-5

Typeset in 10.5/14 pt Sabon

Printed and bound in England by
J.H. Haynes & Co. Ltd, Sparkford

Front cover: Commandos wait for orders on Sword Beach. *(Imperial War Museum [IWM] B5090)*

Page 1: Centaur tank on display behind Sword Beach at la Brèche. *(Author)*

Page 3: A Landing Craft Infantry (Small) approaches Queen Red Beach to the left of strongpoint Cod. *(IWM B5102)*

Page 7: Panzer IV from 21st Panzer Division. *(Bundesarchiv 101/493/3365/27)*

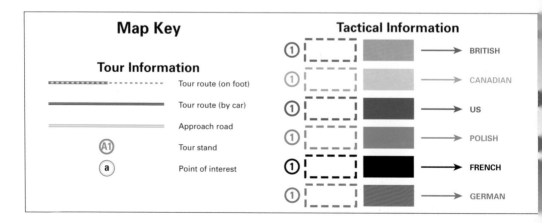

Map Key

Tour Information

···············------------ Tour route (on foot)

———————— Tour route (by car)

———————— Approach road

(A1) Tour stand

(a) Point of interest

Tactical Information

① ⌐ ⌐ ⌐ ➔ BRITISH

① ⌐ ⌐ ⌐ ➔ CANADIAN

① ⌐ ⌐ ⌐ ➔ US

① ⌐ ⌐ ⌐ ➔ POLISH

① ⌐ ⌐ ⌐ ➔ FRENCH

① ⌐ ⌐ ⌐ ➔ GERMAN

CONTENTS

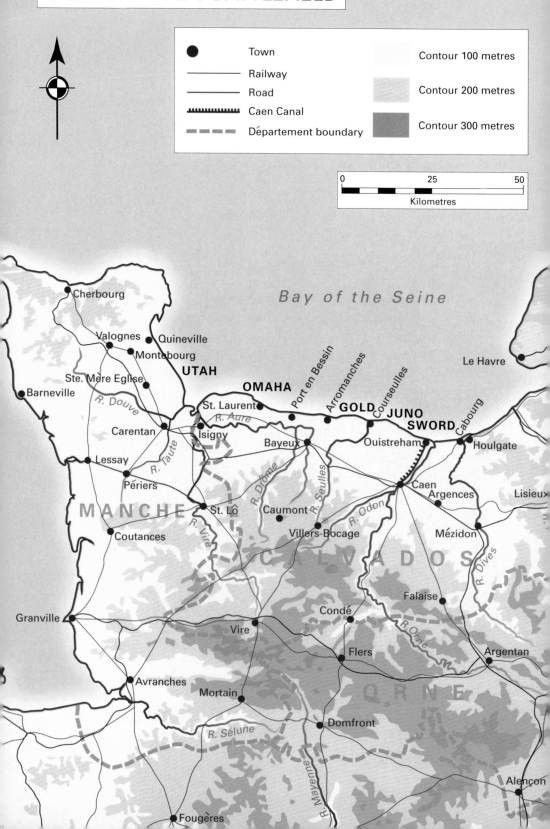

THE NORMANDY BATTLEFIELD

●	Town		Contour 100 metres
	Railway		Contour 200 metres
	Road		Contour 300 metres
	Caen Canal		
	Département boundary		

0   25   50
Kilometres

Bay of the Seine

Cherbourg

Valognes   Quineville
Montebourg

Ste. Mère Eglise   UTAH

Barneville   OMAHA   Port en Bessin   Arromanches   Le Havre

R. Douve   St. Laurent   Courseulles

Carentan   R. Aure   GOLD   JUNO
Isigny   SWORD

Lessay   R. Taute   Bayeux   Ouistreham   Houlgate   Cabourg

Périers   St. Lô   Caumont   R. Seulles   Caen   Argences
MANCHE   R. Drôme   R. Odon   Lisieux

Coutances   R. Vire   Villers-Bocage   Mézidon

CALVADOS   R. Dives

Granville   Condé   Falaise

Vire   R. Orne   ORNE
Avranches   Flers   Argentan

Mortain

R. Séline   Domfront   R. Mayenne

Alençon

Fougères

PART ONE

INTRODUCTION

BATTLE ZONE NORMANDY

The Battle of Normandy was one of the greatest military clashes of all time. From late 1943, when the Allies appointed their senior commanders and began the air operations that were such a vital preliminary to the invasion, until the end of August 1944, it pitted against one another several of the most powerful nations on earth, as well as some of their most brilliant minds. When it was won, it changed the world forever. The price was high, but for anybody who values the principles of freedom and democracy, it is difficult to conclude that it was one not worth paying.

I first visited Lower Normandy in 1994, a year after I joined the War Studies Department at the Royal Military Academy Sandhurst (RMAS). With the 50th anniversary of D-Day looming, it was decided that the British Army would be represented at several major ceremonies by one of the RMAS's officer cadet companies. It was also suggested that the cadets should visit some of the battlefields, not least to bring home to them the significance of why they were there. Thus, at the start of June 1994, I found myself as one of a small team of military and civilian directing staff flying with the cadets in a draughty and noisy Hercules transport to visit the beaches and fields of Calvados, in my case for the first time.

I was hooked. Having met some of the veterans and seen the ground over which they fought – and where many of their friends died – I was determined to go back. Fortunately, the Army encourages battlefield touring as part of its soldiers' education, and on numerous occasions since 1994 I have been privileged to return to Normandy, often to visit new sites. In the process I have learned a vast amount, both from my colleagues (several of whom are contributors to this series) and from my enthusiastic and sometimes tri-service audiences, whose professional insights and penetrating questions have frequently made me re-examine my own assumptions and prejudices. Perhaps inevitably, especially when standing in one of Normandy's beautifully-maintained Commonwealth War Graves Commission cemeteries, I have also found myself deeply moved by the critical events that took place there in the summer of 1944.

'Battle Zone Normandy' was conceived by Jonathan Falconer, Commissioning Editor at Sutton Publishing, in 2001. Why not, he suggested, bring together recent academic research – some of which challenges the general perception of what happened on and after 6 June 1944 – with a perspective based on familiarity with the ground itself? We agreed that the opportunity existed for a series that would set out to combine detailed and accurate narratives, based mostly on primary sources, with illustrated guides to the ground itself, which could be used either in the field (sometimes quite literally), or by the armchair explorer. The book in your hands is the product of that agreement.

The 'Battle Zone Normandy' series consists of 14 volumes, covering most of the major and many of the minor engagements that went together to create the Battle of Normandy. The first six books deal with the airborne and amphibious landings on 6 June 1944, and with the struggle to create the firm lodgement that was the prerequisite for eventual Allied victory. Five further volumes cover some of the critical battles that followed, as the Allies' plans unravelled and they were forced to improvise a battle very different from that originally intended. Finally, the last three titles in the series examine the fruits of the bitter attritional struggle of June and July 1944, as the Allies irrupted through the German lines or drove them back in fierce fighting. The series ends, logically enough, with the devastation of the German armed forces in the 'Falaise Pocket' in late August.

Whether you use these books while visiting Normandy, or to experience the battlefields vicariously, we hope you will find them as interesting to read as we did to research and write. Far from the inevitable victory that is sometimes represented, D-Day and the ensuing battles were full of hazards and unpredictability. Contrary to the view often expressed, had the invasion failed, it is far from certain that a second attempt could have been mounted. Remember this, and the significance of the contents of this book, not least for your life today, will be the more obvious.

Dr Simon Trew
Royal Military Academy Sandhurst
December 2003

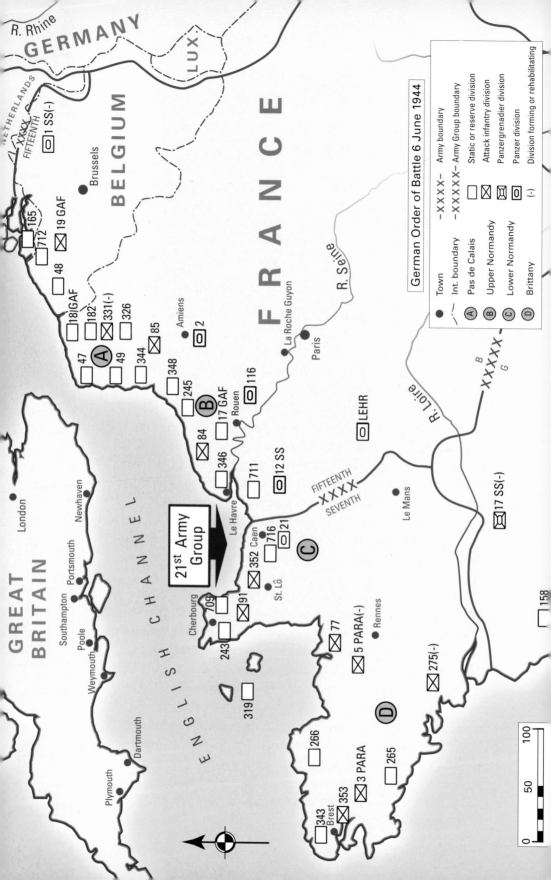

GERMANY
R. Rhine
LUX
NETHERLANDS
XXXX FIFTEENTH
1 SS(-)
BELGIUM
Brussels
165
712
19 GAF
48
18 GAF
182
331(-)
326
A
Amiens
47
49
344
85
2
FRANCE
R. Seine
La Roche Guyon
Paris
348
245
B
17 GAF
116
84
Rouen
346
711
12 SS
LEHR
R. Loire
XXXXX G
FIFTEENTH
XXXX
SEVENTH
Le Mans
17 SS(-)
Le Havre
21st Army Group
716
21
352
Caen
C
St. Lô
709
91
Cherbourg
243
77
Rennes
5 PARA(-)
275(-)
319
D
GREAT BRITAIN
London
Newhaven
Portsmouth
Southampton
Poole
Weymouth
Dartmouth
Plymouth
ENGLISH CHANNEL
266
353
Brest
343
3 PARA
265
158

German Order of Battle 6 June 1944

● Town	–XXXX– Army boundary
Int. boundary	–XXXXX– Army Group boundary
	☐ Static or reserve division
	☒ Attack infantry division
	☒☒ Panzergrenadier division
Ⓐ Pas de Calais	◻ Panzer division
Ⓑ Upper Normandy	(-) Division forming or rehabilitating
Ⓒ Lower Normandy	
Ⓓ Brittany	

0 50 100

FOREWORD

The Royal Anglian Regiment formed on 1 September 1964. On our Colours we carry with great pride 98 of the 299 hard-earned battle honours of our eight forebear Regiments. One of those is 'Normandy Landing'. Battalions of four of our forebear Regiments were involved in this epic operation. Three of them, 1st Suffolks (part of 8th Infantry Brigade, which I had the honour to command in a very different campaign 46 years later), 1st Royal Norfolks, and 2nd Lincolns, were part of 3rd Infantry Division and landed over Sword Beach, the subject of this book. The fourth, 2nd Essex, were part of 56th Independent Infantry Brigade and landed on Gold Beach to liberate Bayeux on D+1.

Normandy continues to be of great importance to our Regiment. Each year veterans of the forebear Regiments, often with representation from our Regular and Territorial battalions, return to France to honour those who fought and died, and to sustain friendships developed over the years with the community. Thanks to the generosity of Madame Suzanne Lenauld, The Suffolk Regiment Association owns part of the Hillman Bunker, and established a memorial there in 1989. The Royal Norfolk Regiment Association has memorials further inland, at Pavée (Sourdevalle) where Corporal Sidney Bates won his posthumous VC, and Grimbosq, where Captain David Jamieson won his VC. The Essex Regiment Association unveiled their memorial in Bayeux on 7 June 2001 with strong Regimental representation.

A privilege enjoyed by a number of our officers and NCOs over the years has been to visit these battlefields accompanied by our veterans who fought there. For those who have little or no experience of war-fighting operations, such visits are invaluable. They help us to understand the harsh realities of combat and what it takes, whether as a soldier, NCO or junior officer in a section, platoon or company, or as a battalion or formation commander, to fight, endure and win. This book extends that privilege to the reader.

The operations covered are full of interest at many different levels. The challenge of making an assault landing on a hostile, fortified shore defended by a first-rate enemy was formidable. The feat of joint planning, organisation, training, technical and logistical support that made it possible was extraordinary. The psychology of men returning to France to engage the main enemy, with whom their fathers had fought for more than four bloody years in 1914–18 and who had defeated them decisively in 1940, bears reflection. Consideration should be given to how the plans, executed with courage and determination, but disrupted by casualties, confusion and the unexpected, worked out in reality, with greater or lesser success. The bitter tactical battles of companies, platoons and individuals show the reality of close combat. Also shown are the dilemmas of battalion and brigade commanders with the mission of reaching Caen and linking up with the airborne landings on D-Day, yet very conscious of the risk of over-extending their largely inexperienced troops against an enemy whose capacity for vicious counter-attack was well known.

For the readers who undertake the recommended tours of the battle zone, there is the opportunity to reflect upon these and many other issues. There are also constant reminders of the courage, comradeship and sacrifice of those who fought, and of the terrible cost of war.

Major-General J.C.B. Sutherell, CB, CBE
Colonel, The Royal Anglian Regiment

PART TWO

HISTORY

CHAPTER I

OPERATION OVERLORD AND SWORD BEACH

By the end of 1942 it was clear to most British and American leaders that a powerful force would eventually have to be landed on the continent of Europe to strike at the heart of Hitler's Germany. To end the war the fight would need to be taken to the gates of Berlin itself and the Nazi Empire destroyed in its homeland. Everything else, the fighting in other theatres, the naval campaigns, the bombing war, secret operations and resistance networks, important as each of them were to the war effort, was all undertaken to keep the Germans engaged and wear them down whilst preparations were made for this one

Above: Tank landing craft moored alongside 101 Berth in Southampton Docks prior to D-Day. *(IWM A23730)*

Page 13: Men of one of the beach groups wading ashore on Sword Beach during the follow-up waves on D-Day. 5th and 6th Beach Groups were responsible for organising the logistics of the landings, arranging such things as local defence, fuel depots, general transport, medical facilities, engineering and port operating equipment. *(IWM B5004)*

event. The war would never be over until Allied soldiers occupied every square metre of the Third Reich and Hitler had been removed from power. Britain, the United States and the Soviet Union would accept nothing short of unconditional surrender.

Crews from C Squadron, 13th/18th Hussars, busy with their final preparations a week before the invasion. C Squadron was not equipped with Duplex Drive tanks and was landed 'dry' from LCTs during the follow-up waves. *(IWM H38970)*

The route into Germany for the western Allies would have to begin in Britain and it was here that the bulk of their forces were concentrated. By the spring of 1944, the USA had assembled over 1.5 million men in the country. Britain had 1.7 million men in uniform with the home-based forces and these numbers were swelled by 220,000 troops from the Commonwealth (mainly Canadians), together with thousands of escapees from territories occupied by Germany. To this pool of manpower was added the manufacturing output of the free world. Britain had become a vast armed camp of men and matériel readying itself for the great crusade.

Commandos of 1st Special Service Brigade leave their holding camp on Southampton Common and begin their move to Warsash on the River Hamble to start their embarkation for Normandy. *(IWM BU1178)*

Across the English Channel, the Germans were also preparing for the inevitable invasion. Hitler's power was on the wane. He knew that an invasion was coming, but he did not know when it would happen or where the blow would fall. In contrast, the Allies had the advantage of choosing exactly when and where their seaborne attack would strike.

The shortest route for the Allies to take would be across the narrow section of the English Channel near the Pas de Calais. To counter this obvious threat the Germans concentrated the strongest of their coastal defences there. However, the obvious is not necessarily the most effective or the most logical and the Germans had also to be prepared for the Allied invasion to strike at almost any point along their occupied coastline from Norway to Spain. In the event the Allies chose Lower Normandy as their preferred location for three main reasons. First, Normandy could be reached by a relatively short Channel crossing from southern England; second, its beaches were within the range of air cover of Allied fighters; and third, the German defences at the proposed location were not as formidable as those in the Calais area.

With the area of Lower Normandy selected as the site of the invasion, detailed planning could begin on the locations of the landing beaches and the objectives of the initial assault. The strategy finally agreed upon was to attack the coast on five beaches stretching from the base of the Cotentin Peninsula to the mouth of the River Orne. American troops would land on two beaches in the west, code-named 'Utah' and 'Omaha', while the British and Canadians would land on three beaches in the east of the invasion area, at 'Gold', 'Juno' and 'Sword'. After gaining a secure lodgement, the forces from the American beaches would combine to seal off the Cotentin Peninsula and move north to capture the port of Cherbourg. The British and Canadians would link up with the Americans to develop a continuous beachhead and to enlarge the landings to a depth sufficient to accommodate supply bases from which further operations could be conducted.

Crucial to the security of the beachhead was the early capture of Caen, situated 12 kilometres (km) inland of the eastern side of the amphibious landings. Caen was the centre of an important network of roads decisive to the Allied exploitation of the lodgement or to German attempts to launch effective counter-attacks. To the south of the town, open flat countryside would be ideal for launching an armoured breakout. The capture of Caen and the seizing of a sizeable lodgement in this important eastern sector would be accomplished from a landing beach close to the mouth of the River Orne. This was Sword Beach. The British 3rd Infantry Division was given the task of landing on Sword, gaining a beachhead and seizing Caen on the day of the invasion.

It required much organisation to formulate a plan for the security of the left flank of the landings and the early capture of Caen. The town lies inland along the River Orne and its adjacent canal. These waterways would form an immediate barrier to any eastwards expansion of the beachhead. Crossing places over the Orne would have to be quickly captured and held against

Commandos go aboard their Landing Craft Infantry (Small) at Warsash near Southampton on the afternoon of 5 June. These wooden craft were to take them across the Channel right to Queen sector of Sword Beach. *(IWM H39043)*

counter-attack as security for further operations. The German reserves would also have to be kept as far as possible from this side of the landings to prevent them interfering with the build-up of the lodgement over Sword Beach. It was therefore decided that an airborne division would be dropped on the eastern side of the Orne, prior to the amphibious assault, to seize the crossing places and control the eastern flank of the invasion area. British 6th Airborne Division was allocated these objectives, to be carried out during the night before the invasion.

On the western flank of the proposed landings, the same tasks of flank protection were given to US airborne forces. Between the two secured flanks, other Allied divisions would land and seize the centre of the lodgement over Omaha, Gold and Juno Beaches. Further divisions would follow soon after to enlarge the beachhead and drive inland.

Nobody in the Allied camp underestimated the dangers of landing troops over open beaches against an entrenched and well-prepared enemy. Some sceptics predicted a bloodbath, with losses so high that the invasion forces would have to be withdrawn. These opinions were clouded by the experiences suffered during the abortive attack on the port of Dieppe in August 1942. Over 50 per cent of the forces that participated in that raid were either killed or captured. Many lessons were learned from the débâcle, most of which were implemented in time for D-Day.

The Dieppe raid showed that new techniques would have to be developed to deal with fixed fortifications. Special armoured vehicles would be needed to attack concrete emplacements and to overcome beach obstacles. The roles of the navy and air force would also need to be more effectual, with air and sea support being integrated with the requirements of the men on the ground. The size of the assault was also crucial with enough landing craft being made available to put a strong force ashore in one lift. The Germans had to be struck by an overwhelming force, all co-ordinated to hit in one massive assault. The first waves ashore had to break through the crust of beach defences and get off the shore line to allow follow-up waves to deploy.

The Germans' success in repulsing the landings at Dieppe contributed to their ultimate defeat, for Hitler saw the victory as a vindication of his chosen strategy to deal with a seaborne invasion. Strong fixed defences manned by even average military personnel had proved to be difficult to penetrate from the sea.

Vehicles and tanks of the 13th/18th Hussars on passage to Normandy. The three men in the centre are beach group personnel, recognisable from the white bands around their steel helmets. *(IWM B5110)*

The attackers at Dieppe had been stopped on the beaches and then decimated by weapons housed in virtually indestructible concrete bunkers overlooking all likely landing places. Any gaps in the defence line were sealed by mobile troops located close by. Hitler believed that this was how an invasion could be stopped. He ordered the building of an impregnable 'Atlantic Wall' against which his enemies would dash themselves to pieces.

One of the major conclusions the Allies gained from the raid on Dieppe was that it would be suicidal to storm a heavily defended port from the sea. A port, nonetheless, had to be operational soon after the landings to deal with the enormous volume of men and matériel that would be needed to support the attacks inland. There were only two ports in Normandy suitable for such an undertaking, Cherbourg and Le Havre. To wait for either of these to be captured and made operational by a landward attack could take a considerable time. The main thrust from the Allied lodgement was also to be southwards, away from these ports, adding to possible delays. The problem of having a suitable harbour available was solved by the ingenious idea of building two gigantic artificial harbours in Britain, code-named

An RAF Typhoon fighter-bomber being armed by its servicing crew on an advanced landing ground in Normandy. Capturing areas where such airfields could be built was an important early objective for the invasion. *(IWM CL157)*

'Mulberry', and towing them across the Channel to site them off the Normandy coast. In the event both of these artificial harbours were operational within 12 days of the invasion.

In the two years that followed Dieppe, the Germans continued to strengthen the shore defences of northern Europe, albeit sometimes half-heartedly. In November 1943 considerable impetus was given to this building programme by the appointment of *Generalfeldmarschall* (Field Marshal) Erwin Rommel to command Army Group B in France and the Low Countries and to be responsible for improving the Atlantic Wall. Rommel believed that an invasion had to be stopped on the beaches. Any major landing should be attacked by armour before it could become effective. Rommel therefore advocated that panzer forces should be stationed within striking distance of the sea so that they could attack on the day invaders came ashore.

This view was not shared, however, by all of German high command. Field Marshal Gerd von Rundstedt, Commander-in-Chief West and Rommel's nominal superior, advocated keeping the armoured divisions away from the coast to watch how any landing might develop. Then, at a time and place of his choosing, he would launch a massive armoured attack against the Allied forces as they moved inland and annihilate them and their lodgement. Other senior officers agreed with this view.

Hitler wavered between these two tactical options. He placed great reliance on the strength of his Atlantic Wall, but was also an advocate of massed panzer attacks. He decided on a compromise: the bulk of the armour would be stationed inland and kept under his control, whilst three armoured divisions would be kept close to the Channel, one in Lower Normandy (21st Panzer Division near Caen), one near the Pas de Calais (2nd Panzer Division at Amiens) and one near Paris (116th Panzer Division). These would be placed under Rommel's control in Army Group B, able to react immediately to any landings. This decision put 21st Panzer Division within striking distance of Sword Beach on D-Day.

CHAPTER 2

THE OPPOSING ARMIES AND THEIR COMMANDERS

In December 1943 General Dwight D. Eisenhower was appointed Supreme Commander Allied Expeditionary Force to lead the invasion of Europe, with General Sir Bernard Montgomery commanding his armies in the field as head of 21st Army Group. Montgomery would head all the land forces used in the invasion, while Eisenhower controlled the overall prosecution of the war in north-west Europe. The plan for the operation was code-named 'Overlord' and it had been drawn up prior to both taking up their appointments. The first version of the plan was based on various factors, not least the limited number of landing craft then available in Britain. Eisenhower and Montgomery insisted that the number of divisions used in the initial amphibious assault be increased to five and the number of beaches they were to land over also be enlarged. The two generals eventually got their way.

Under the new plan, two separate armies would undertake the attack and begin the initial drive inland. Other armies would be introduced into the battle as more territory was taken and the lodgement expanded. Lieutenant General Omar N. Bradley commanded American forces for Overlord. His First US Army would land on Utah and Omaha Beaches in the west, while

Lieutenant-General (Lt-Gen) Miles Dempsey landed British Second Army over the beaches on the eastern side of the attack.

Lt-Gen Dempsey was one of Montgomery's favourite subordinates and had fought with him in many of his greatest battles. Dempsey had commanded a brigade at Dunkirk, a division in England and a corps in North Africa, Sicily and Italy. At Montgomery's insistence, Dempsey was brought home to train and command Second Army for the invasion. Dempsey's troops would land over Gold, Juno and Sword Beaches.

Dempsey's opposite number in the German Army, responsible for the area of northern France containing the invasion area, was *Generaloberst* (Colonel-General) Friedrich Dollmann. In contrast to Dempsey, Dollmann had become rather out of touch with the war. He had been in command of German Seventh Army since 1939 and had not seen action since the end of the French campaign in 1940. For the next four years he and his army remained in France as occupation troops, languishing in a mostly peaceful landscape. Under his command coast defences tended to remain a low priority, for Dollmann, like von Rundstedt, was inclined to think that any invasion could best be defeated by an overwhelming tank attack once it was well inside the country. Dollmann's time in France had blunted his ability to grasp the

The Overlord team: (*L to R*) Lieutenant General Bradley, First (US) Army; Admiral Ramsay, Naval Force Commander; Air Chief Marshal Sir Arthur Tedder, Deputy Supreme Commander; General Eisenhower, Supreme Commander; General Montgomery, 21st Army Group; Air Chief Marshal Sir Trafford Leigh-Mallory, Air Force Commander; and Lieutenant General Walter Bedell Smith, Chief of Staff to Supreme Commander. *(IWM CH12109)*

changes that had occurred in warfare, most importantly knowledge of the use of panzer troops and an understanding of the overwhelming superiority of the Allied air forces.

The coast of Calvados, upon which Second Army's landings were to take place, was within the sector controlled by German LXXXIV Corps, commanded by *General der Artillerie* (General of Artillery) Erich Marcks, an officer of great bravery and experience. Marcks had seen action in the First World War and again since 1939. He had served in the Polish campaign and later became one of the planners for Operation 'Barbarossa', the invasion of Russia. He was badly wounded on the Eastern Front in 1942 and lost a leg. When he returned to active service in August 1943, he was promoted to take over LXXXIV Corps and became liable for the defence of some 385 km of French coast.

The Allied corps commander responsible for both Juno and Sword Beaches was Lt-Gen John Crocker, commander of British I Corps. Crocker was a tank man who had commanded an armoured brigade in France in 1940, an armoured division in England in 1941 and a corps in Tunisia in 1943. He was brought home from Africa in August 1943 to take over I Corps and prepare it for the invasion. His knowledge of the use of armour, together with his proven ability as a trainer of men, made him perfectly suited for the task.

Lt-Gens John Crocker of British I Corps (*left*) and Miles Dempsey, of British Second Army. (*IWM B5325*)

Sword Beach was located to the west of the tiny port of Ouistreham at the mouth of the River Orne, just 12 km from Caen. If the British planners had quickly identified the capture of Caen as the key to the successful exploitation of the landings on Sword Beach, then it was not surprising that the Germans had also recognised the town as being the cornerstone of their defence of Normandy. Rommel therefore garrisoned 21st Panzer Division close to the town for immediate commitment should a landing take place on the beaches to the north.

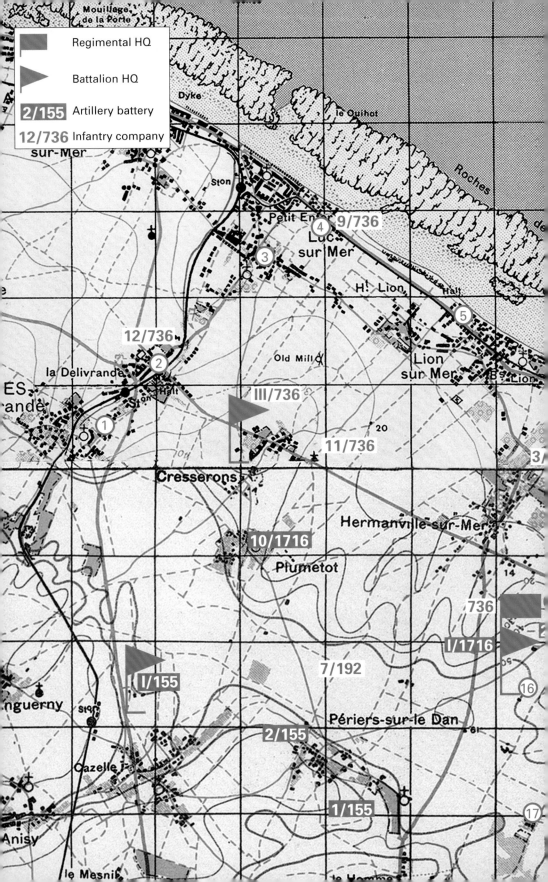

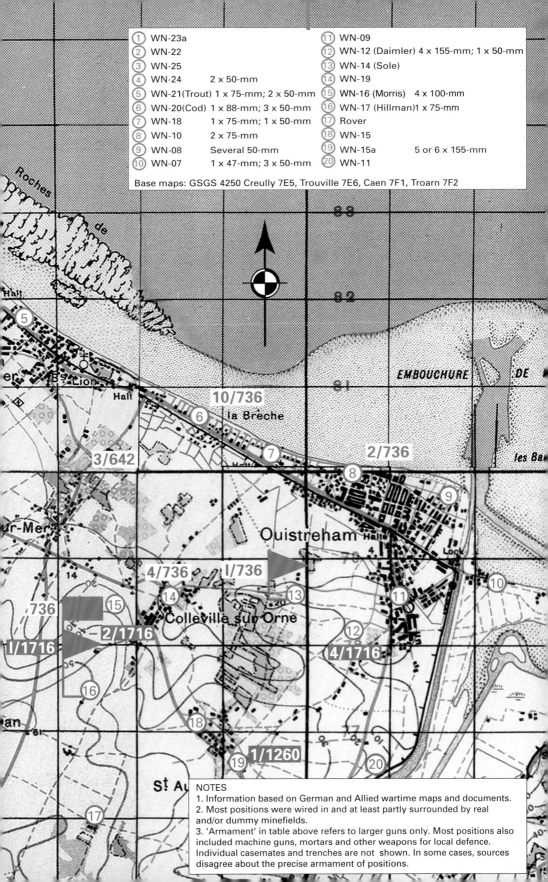

① WN-23a
② WN-22
③ WN-25
④ WN-24   2 x 50-mm
⑤ WN-21(Trout) 1 x 75-mm; 2 x 50-mm
⑥ WN-20(Cod)   1 x 88-mm; 3 x 50-mm
⑦ WN-18   1 x 75-mm; 1 x 50-mm
⑧ WN-10   2 x 75-mm
⑨ WN-08   Several 50-mm
⑩ WN-07   1 x 47-mm; 3 x 50-mm

⑪ WN-09
⑫ WN-12 (Daimler) 4 x 155-mm; 1 x 50-mm
⑬ WN-14 (Sole)
⑭ WN-19
⑮ WN-16 (Morris) 4 x 100-mm
⑯ WN-17 (Hillman)1 x 75-mm
⑰ Rover
⑱ WN-15
⑲ WN-15a   5 or 6 x 155-mm
⑳ WN-11

Base maps: GSGS 4250 Creully 7E5, Trouville 7E6, Caen 7F1, Troarn 7F2

NOTES
1. Information based on German and Allied wartime maps and documents.
2. Most positions were wired in and at least partly surrounded by real and/or dummy minefields.
3. 'Armament' in table above refers to larger guns only. Most positions also included machine guns, mortars and other weapons for local defence. Individual casemates and trenches are not shown. In some cases, sources disagree about the precise armament of positions.

The task of capturing Caen was given to the same division as was to assault Sword Beach, British 3rd Infantry Division. The commander of the division was Major-General (Maj-Gen) Tom Rennie, a Scotsman from the Black Watch. Rennie had been captured in France in 1940 while serving with his regiment as part of 51st (Highland) Division, but escaped and made his way home. He then commanded a battalion in North Africa and later a brigade of 51st (Highland) Division. He was promoted to major-general in 1943 and took over 3rd Infantry Division to prepare it for the invasion. By D-Day, the division was fully trained in all aspects of amphibious assault, but most of its men were not seasoned in combat. Morale was, nonetheless, very high for the men felt that they were well trained and equipped for the tasks ahead. (*See pp. 28–29 for full 3rd Division order of battle.*)

The American-made Priest self-propelled gun was the main weapon of 3rd Infantry Division's field artillery regiments. This example is on display in the grounds of the Atlantic Wall Museum at Ouistreham. *(Author)*

Opposing Rennie's division on Sword Beach was *Generalleutnant* (GenLt) Wilhelm Richter with his 716th Infantry Division. Richter was an artilleryman and a veteran of the First World War. He had fought in the campaigns in Poland, Belgium and France in 1939–40, then in Russia in 1941–43. In April 1943 he was put in charge of 716th Infantry Division and given the task of holding the coastal sector north of Caen.

The 716th Infantry Division was a static division raised in the

Wilhelm Richter, commander of 716th Infantry Division (before he was promoted to general). *(Private Collection/Archives du Mémorial de Caen)*

area of Bielefeld in Germany's *Wehrkreis* (Military District) VI. The division consisted of two regiments, each with three battalions. 726th Grenadier Regiment was commanded by *Oberst* (Colonel) Walter Korfes (most of this regiment was under command of 352nd Infantry Division on D-Day) and 736th Grenadier Regiment by *Oberst* Ludwig Krug. Each of these regiments was supplemented with a battalion of troops recruited in Russia. Known as *Ost* (East) battalions, such units usually contained about 1,000 men, mostly former Soviet prisoners of war. They were viewed with suspicion by German commanders who doubted their effectiveness in battle. 439th *Ost* Battalion joined with 726th Grenadier Regiment, and 642nd *Ost* Battalion was placed in 736th Grenadier Regiment. The division's artillery component, 1716th Artillery Regiment, contained three battalions, one of which was also allocated to 352nd Division. Also attached to the division were the usual support units that were required to keep the unit operational, such as engineers, anti-tank, signals and supply troops. Being designated a 'static' division, it was provided with a minimum of motor vehicles, and had to make great use of horses as a means of transport.

During its period of garrison duties and coast defence, the division had also been stripped of many of its younger men to provide reinforcements for the units being decimated in Russia. These men were often replaced by older men and conscripted foreigners who diluted the morale and efficiency of the formation. Nevertheless, from autumn 1943 the division received considerable reinforcement, including many experienced officers and NCOs. Together with an influx of new equipment, this did much to improve its fighting power.

GenLt Richter's responsibility stretched from Franceville Plage, across the mouth of the River Orne westwards to la Rivière. This covered both Sword and Juno Beaches and part of Gold Beach, a distance of about 45 km. It is not surprising, then, that his troops

Order of Battle: British 3rd Infantry Division
6 JUNE 1944

General Officer Commanding: *Major-General T.G. Rennie*

8th Infantry Brigade
1st Battalion, The Suffolk Regiment   (abbreviated as *1 Suffolks*)
2nd Battalion, The East Yorkshire Regiment   (*2 E Yorks*)
1st Battalion, The South Lancashire Regiment   (*1 S Lancs*)

9th Infantry Brigade
2nd Battalion, The Lincolnshire Regiment   (*2 Lincolns*)
1st Battalion, The King's Own Scottish Borderers   (*1 KOSB*)
2nd Battalion, The Royal Ulster Rifles   (*2 RUR*)

185th Infantry Brigade
2nd Battalion, The Royal Warwickshire Regiment   (*2 Warwicks*)
1st Battalion, The Royal Norfolk Regiment   (*1 Norfolks*)
2nd Battalion, The King's Shropshire Light Infantry   (*2 KSLI*)

Divisional Troops

Machine Gun and Heavy Mortar Battalion
2nd Battalion, The Middlesex Regiment   (*2 Middlesex*)

Royal Artillery
7th Field Regiment (9th, 16th and 17th/43rd Field Batteries)
33rd Field Regiment (101st, 109th and 113th/114th Field Batteries)
76th Field Regiment (302nd, 303rd and 354th Field Batteries)
20th Anti-tank Regiment (41st, 45th, 67th and 101st Anti-tank Batteries)

Royal Engineers
17th, 246th and 253rd Field Companies

Medical
8th, 9th and 223rd Field Ambulances

Royal Signals
3rd Division Signals

Provost Company
3rd Division Provost Company

Armoured Support Attached to 3rd Infantry Division

27th Independent Armoured Brigade
13th/18th Royal Hussars
1st East Riding Yeomanry
The Staffordshire Yeomanry

Formations Attached to 3rd Infantry Division for the Assault

1st Special Service Brigade
No. 3 Commando
No. 4 Commando
No. 6 Commando
No. 45 (Royal Marine) Commando

4th Special Service Brigade
No. 41 (Royal Marine) Commando

Royal Marines
5th Independent Armoured Support Battery

Royal Armoured Corps
A Squadron, 22nd Dragoons

Royal Engineers
HQ 5th Engineer Assault Regiment
77th and 79th Assault Squadrons
71st and 263rd Field Companies
629th Field Squadron

Royal Artillery
HQ 53rd Medium Battery
218th Battery, 73rd Light Anti-aircraft Regiment
322nd Battery, 93rd Light Anti-aircraft Regiment
B Flight, 652nd Air Observation Point Squadron

RASC
106th Brigade Company
90th Armoured Brigade Company

'Phantom'
GHQ Liaison Regiment

Sub-Area Units Under Command for Assault Phase

Beach Protection Infantry
5th Battalion, The King's Regiment
1st Battalion, The Buckinghamshire Regiment

Royal Engineers
84th and 91st Field Companies
8th and 9th Stores Sections
50th Mechanised Equipment Section
9th, 999th and 1028th Port Operation Companies
940th Inland Water Transport Operating Company

RASC
21st Transport Column
39th, 101st, 299th, 633rd Transport Companies
96th and 138th Detail Issue Depots
237th and 238th Petrol Depots

Medical
16th Casualty Clearing Station
9th, 12th, 20th, 21st and 30th Field Dressing Stations

Ordnance
11th and 12th Ordnance Beach Detachments
44th Ordnance Ammunition Company

REME
20th and 21st Beach Recovery Sections

Provost
241st and 245th Provost Companies

Labour
53rd, 85th, 102nd, 129th, 149th, 267th, 292nd and 303rd Pioneer
Companies, Pioneer Corps

HISTORY

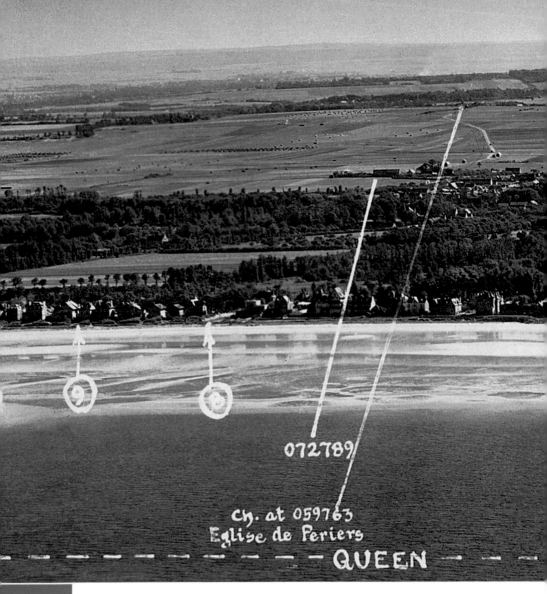

072789

Ch. at 059763
Eglise de Periers

QUEEN

were rather thin on the ground – Richter later described them as being spaced out like a string of pearls. The sector of the division's line along Sword Beach was held by elements of 736th Grenadier Regiment, which had two battalions in the division's 45 km of coastal defences and one in reserve.

The other division that would bar British 3rd Infantry Division's advance from Sword Beach to its final objectives was 21st Panzer Division, commanded by *Generalmajor* (GenMaj) Edgar Feuchtinger. This division had been reformed in July 1943 after the original unit had been destroyed in Tunisia. The equipment of the division was of variable quality. Some of its tanks were obsolete French models and its transport was mostly

Oblique aerial photograph taken before the invasion of the section of Sword Beach to the right of Queen White sector. The villas along the seafront are between la Brèche d'Hermanville and Lion-sur-Mer. Hermanville is in the centre of the picture, with Périers Ridge running across the middle distance. (IWM MH1996)

captured French vehicles. The division's main striking force was 100th Panzer Regiment (then being re-designated as 22nd Panzer Regiment, although still appearing on some German maps of 5 June by the previous title) and the 125th and 192nd Panzer-grenadier Regiments, all of which had two battalions instead of the more usual three. The 155th Panzer Artillery Regiment had three battalions and there was in addition a combat engineer battalion (220th), an anti-tank battalion, an anti-aircraft battalion and a reconnaissance battalion.

GenMaj Feuchtinger was an artilleryman and a veteran of the First World War. He became friendly with Hitler during the rise of the Nazi Party in the 1930s. At the outbreak of war he commanded 227th Artillery Regiment and fought in the 1940 battles in the Netherlands, Belgium and France, before serving with his regiment in Russia where he was wounded. In 1943 he was given command of the 21st Panzer Division, even though he had no knowledge of armoured warfare. It is thought he obtained this promotion through his Nazi Party connections.

Other miscellaneous units provided more personnel to the defences. These included 931st Mobile Brigade and companies of Seventh Army support units.

HISTORY

When 3rd Infantry Division fought its way ashore on 6 June, it was one of the most powerful divisions that had ever left Britain. To help blast its way through the Atlantic Wall, it had a number of specialised units attached to it. It was known that the beach itself was covered with obstacles and explosives between the high and low water marks, all well sited so as to sink or damage landing craft as they came in to the shore. Welded sections of railway lines, steel and concrete tetrahedrons, stakes topped with mines, and complicated steel traps littered the sands. All of these would have to be neutralised or avoided if the craft were to make a safe landing. Parties of Royal Engineers and naval frogmen would land with the main assault to try to clear paths through the obstacles ahead of the follow-up landing craft. The timing of the assault would be midway between low and high tides. This would leave most of the beach defences exposed and avoidable (they had mostly been positioned on the assumption that the Allies would land at high tide), whilst leaving a lesser number covered by water to be neutralised. It would also mean a shorter width of open beach for the infantry to cross before they got amongst the German defences than if the attack took place at low tide. At the top of the beach a triple belt of barbed wire had been laid to tie together the field fortifications and behind these entanglements were many minefields. Machine-gun posts were sited to fire along the beaches in enfilade, their seaward sides often protected by concrete walls. Anchoring the lines of defences were larger strongpoints housing heavier weapons, usually containing around ten machine guns and one or two 50-mm or 75-mm guns, all housed in concrete bunkers or casemates. These resistance posts were called *Wiederstandnester* (WN) and were mainly sited to cover possible routes inland from the beach.

Once the boats had touched down, the emerging infantry would be at the mercy of machine-gun and mortar fire from the fortified positions. It was crucial to the success of the operation that tanks were already on the beaches supporting the assault troops as they arrived. Specialised armoured vehicles were therefore developed to achieve this. One of the most innovative solutions used was the deployment of Duplex Drive (DD) tanks. These were tanks fitted with watertight flotation screens and propellers. The modifications allowed them to be launched from landing craft well out to sea and then 'swim' inconspicuously the last few thousand metres to the shore, able to emerge from the surf moments before the infantry's assault boats touched down. Once on land the DD tanks would drop their skirts, disengage their propeller drives and function as normal tanks. DD Sherman tanks from 13th/18th Hussars were assigned to 3rd Infantry Division for the Sword assault. This regiment was part of 27th Armoured Brigade and the other two battalions of the brigade – the 1st East Riding Yeomanry and the Staffordshire Yeomanry – would land conventionally with their normal Sherman tanks from tank landing craft (LCTs) with the follow-up waves.

Landing craft, with a Sherman Firefly tank of C Squadron, 13th/18th Hussars, on board, in Portsmouth Harbour prior to setting sail for Normandy. *(IWM B5105)*

Other specialised armour was provided for the landings by the British 79th Armoured Division. This division was formed to undertake a range of specific tasks that would be required during an invasion, including breaching the German defences, clearing gaps through minefields and opening exits from the beaches. 79th Armoured Division had been raised in October 1942 under the command of Maj-Gen Percy Hobart. It contained a variety of strange machines that were known collectively as 'Hobart's Funnies'. Each of these modified tanks was designed to overcome a particular problem. To attack casemates and pill-boxes, a new tank was developed. Based on a Churchill chassis, it was armed

HISTORY

with a short-barrelled spigot mortar capable of firing a heavy block-busting explosive charge against reinforced concrete buildings, shattering the structures with devastating force. This type of tank was known as an Armoured Vehicle Royal Engineers (AVRE). Suitably adapted, the AVRE was also capable of other support functions, such as positioning box girder bridges, dropping fascines in anti-tank ditches and laying rolls of matting to help other vehicles cross soft ground or sand. Manning the AVREs in support of 3rd Infantry Division would be 77th and 79th Squadrons of 5th Assault Regiment, Royal Engineers (RE).

Churchill AVRE tank preserved as a memorial to 41 RM Commando located just outside Lion-sur-Mer on the road to Luc-sur-Mer. *(Author)*

More support from 79th Armoured Division was given by its flail tanks, known as 'Crabs'. These were Sherman gun tanks with a revolving drum anchored to the front on which was attached a number of heavy chains. They were designed to clear minefields. As the tank went forwards with the drum turning, the chains beat the ground ahead of it, exploding any mines in its path. This mine clearing support was provided to 3rd Infantry Division by A Squadron, 22nd Dragoons.

Supporting firepower was also supplied to the landings by the other services. A programme of bombing by the Royal Air Force (RAF) and United States Army Air Force (USAAF) had been implemented since well before the invasion to seal off Normandy from the rest of France. Railway lines and marshalling yards were attacked and bridges blown over rivers and canals to frustrate military traffic. This disruption was intended to slow down the rate at which the Germans could bring reinforcements into the invasion area. More immediate assistance was provided through

HISTORY

Naval Assault Group S3 Carrying Attack Landings to Sword Beach

Headquarters:	HMS *Vernon*, Portsmouth
Assault Group HQ Ship:	HMS *Goathland*

Landing Ships Infantry (Large)	LSI (L) – Troop Transports
HMS *Glenearn*	
435th Assault Flotilla	12 Landing Craft Assault (LCA)
543rd Assault Flotilla	12 LCA
HMS *Empire Battleaxe*	
537th Assault Flotilla	18 LCA
HMS *Empire Broadsword*	
538th Assault Flotilla	18 LCA
SS *Empire Cutlass*	
536th Assault Flotilla	18 LCA

E Squadron Landing Craft	
261st Landing Craft Infantry (Large) Flotilla	
	5 LCI (L)
14th Landing Craft Tank Flotilla	9 LCT
41st Landing Craft Tank Flotilla	14 LCT
43rd Landing Craft Tank Flotilla	10 LCT
45th Landing Craft Tank Flotilla	10 LCT

Support Squadron	
330th Support Flotilla	4 Landing Craft Flak (LCF)
	3 Landing Craft Gun (LCG)
	1 LCT Concrete Buster (LCT-CB)
32nd LCT Flotilla	14 LCT
38th LCT Flotilla	9 LCT
100th LCT (Armoured) Flotilla	8 LCT(A)
321st LCT (Rocket) Flotilla	5 LCT(R)
392nd Assault Flotilla	9 LCA (Hedgerow)
	2 Landing Craft Personnel (Survey)
704th Assault Flotilla	4 LCP(L), 2 LCP(Sy)
707th Assault Flotilla	12 LCP(L)

the aircraft of the two tactical air forces – the RAF's 2nd Tactical Air Force aiding British Second Army and the USAAF's 9th Air Force helping First US Army. Individual fortifications, anti-tank obstacles, troop concentrations and gun batteries were all targets for Allied fighter-bombers. Strategic bombers also played their part in softening up the defences, with RAF Bomber Command and the US 8th Air Force bombing whole areas adjacent to the landing beaches, flying missions right up until the assault boats were actually completing their run-in to the shore.

Naval support for the invasion was equally impressive. Naval Commander-in-Chief for the sea component of the invasion,

Operation 'Neptune', was Admiral Sir Bertram Ramsay. He had a total of 7,016 vessels under command. The American beaches were supported by the Western Task Force (Rear-Admiral Alan G. Kirk) and the British beaches by the Eastern Task Force (Rear-Admiral Sir Philip Vian). Naval Force S contained the assault forces for Sword Beach under the command of Rear-Admiral A.G. Talbot. Bombarding Force D, supporting Force S, used the heavy guns of battleships, cruisers and monitors to target individual gun batteries which might interfere with the landings from as far away as Le Havre. Destroyers would bombard targets from close in and then Landing Craft Gun – LCG, Landing Craft Flak – LCT(F), Landing Craft Rocket – LCT(R), and Landing Craft Assault (Hedgerow) – LCA(HR) would fire during the run to the shore. Finally there were the self-propelled guns of the division's own artillery regiments and Centaur tanks from the Royal Marine Armoured Support Group firing from the open decks of tank landing craft.

In contrast to the Allies' great show of strength at sea and in the air, the *Kriegsmarine* (German Navy) and the *Luftwaffe* (German Air Force) could muster little in reply. The Channel had been swept of all German naval vessels save for small coastal ships, minesweepers, patrol boats and torpedo boats. *Admiral* Theodore Krancke, C-in-C Naval Group Command West, could only muster 103 light craft between Cherbourg and Boulogne with which to counter Admiral Ramsay's 7,000 vessels. In the air, Field Marshal Hugo Sperrle, commander of 3rd Air Fleet, had only 115 serviceable single-engined fighters with which to protect the whole of France, Belgium and Holland.

CHAPTER 3

THE LANDINGS ON SWORD BEACH

The area of the coastline designated as Sword Beach stretched westwards from the mouth of the River Orne to the east of St-Aubin-sur-Mer. Allied planners divided the beach into four sectors: 'Oboe' from St-Aubin-sur-Mer to Luc-sur-Mer; 'Peter'

The site of strongpoint Cod looking eastwards. The prominent villa on the right of the picture dates from before the war and was incorporated in the western end of the German resistance post. The new footpath on the left marks the line of dunes that ran along the top of the beach. The assault companies of 8th Infantry Brigade landed along this stretch of the shore. *(Author)*

from Luc to Lion-sur-Mer; 'Queen' from Lion to the road leading to Colleville-Montgomery (which was simply Colleville in 1944) at la Brèche d'Hermanville; and 'Roger' from la Brèche to the Orne at Ouistreham. The length of beach selected for the assault was Queen sector and this was further subdivided into areas, Green (west, the Allied right), White (centre) and Red (left). The seaward approaches to Sword Beach generally were over shallow reefs, with the only gap through them of any appreciable depth being a narrow one at la Brèche on Queen sector. Therefore the actual site for the landfall of the assault waves would be over White and Red sections of Queen Beach. This limited the size of the initial assault to one brigade, with two battalions in the attack and one in reserve as the follow-up wave.

In broad terms the orders given to Maj-Gen Rennie for D-Day were to land his division over Queen Red and White Beaches and then advance inland to capture Caen and seize the crossings over the River Orne there. Leading 3rd Infantry Division ashore in the assault wave would be 2 E Yorks and 1 S Lancs of 8th Infantry Brigade. The brigade's other battalion, 1 Suffolks, would land later in the second of the follow-up waves. Landing with this first wave would be the DD tanks of the 13th/18th Hussars and the

specialised armour of 5th Assault Regiment, RE, together with the flail tanks of A Squadron, 22nd Dragoons.

Brigadier E.E. Cass, commander of 8th Infantry Brigade, had been given a number of objectives to complete, the first of which was to carry out the assault over Queen White and Red Beaches and to eliminate the German shore defences on them. 1 S Lancs would then move inland and seize the village of Hermanville and consolidate a defensive position on its southern outskirts to allow other units to pass through. 2 E Yorks would move off the beach south-eastwards and capture the strongpoints WN-14 (code-named 'Sole') and WN-12 ('Daimler'). 1 Suffolks would land behind them and advance southwards to Colleville, then attack strongpoints WN-16 ('Morris') and WN-17 ('Hillman'), before finally moving on to take control of the commanding heights of Périers Ridge. This assault brigade would clear the way for the follow-up brigades to exploit.

A tank landing craft unloads an AVRE from 79th Armoured Division on Sword Beach in the chaos of burning vehicles and German fire. *(IWM B5112)*

Next to land, after 8th Infantry Brigade, was 185th Infantry Brigade commanded by Brigadier K. Smith. This brigade was charged with capturing Caen with its 2 Warwicks, 1 Norfolks and 2 KSLI. Smith was ordered to advance inland out of the beachhead, 'with speed and boldness', with a battle group consisting of 2 KSLI; a troop of 41st Anti-tank Battery in M10 Wolverine self-propelled guns; the Sherman tanks of the Staffordshire Yeomanry; and two troops of flail tanks from A Squadron, 22nd Dragoons. This mobile column, with the infantry travelling on the backs of the tanks, would rush to Caen along the axis Hermanville–Beuville–Biéville–Lébisey, while 1 Norfolks and 2 Warwicks followed the advance on either flank.

The division's reserve brigade was 9th Infantry Brigade, commanded by Brigadier J. Cunningham. It would land behind 185th Infantry Brigade and move initially into an assembly area inland of Lion-sur-Mer. The brigade's main tasks were to provide right flank protection for the division and to link up with the Canadian units moving inland from Juno Beach. If 185th Infantry Brigade failed to take Caen, 9th Infantry Brigade was to attack the town from the west. First, its 2 Lincolns would clear the concentration area and take Plumetot and Cresserons. Then 1 KOSB and 2 RUR would move southwards with the Shermans of the East Riding Yeomanry and occupy the ground to the north-west of Caen around St-Contest and Mâlon, linking up with the Canadians who should by then be close by at Buron.

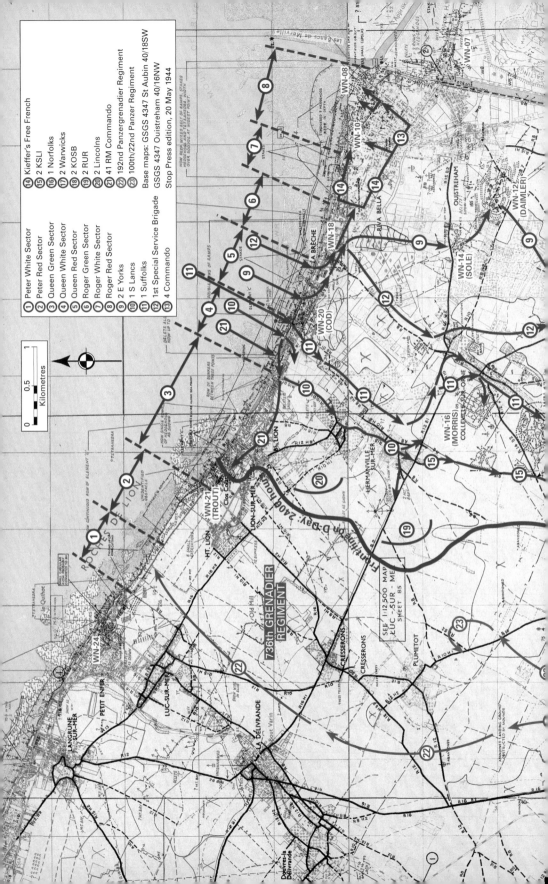

Legend:

1. Peter White Sector
2. Peter Red Sector
3. Queen Green Sector
4. Queen White Sector
5. Queen Red Sector
6. Roger Green Sector
7. Roger White Sector
8. Roger Red Sector
9. 2 E Yorks
10. 1 S Lancs
11. 1 Suffolks
12. 1st Special Service Brigade
13. 4 Commando
14. Kieffer's Free French
15. 2 KSLI
16. 1 Norfolks
17. 2 Warwicks
18. 2 KOSB
19. 2 RUR
20. 2 Lincolns
21. 41 RM Commando
22. 192nd Panzergrenadier Regiment
23. 100th/22nd Panzer Regiment

Base maps: GSGS 4347 St Aubin 40/18SW
GSGS 4347 Ouistreham 40/16NW
Stop Press edition, 20 May 1944

Attached to 3rd Infantry Division for the assault were a number of individual commandos. 1st Special Service Brigade, commanded by Brigadier Lord Lovat, contained four Commandos: Nos. 3, 4 and 6 Army Commandos and No. 45 Royal Marine (RM) Commando. Lovat had two main tasks. The first objective involved 4 Commando, with two French troops of 10 (Inter-Allied) Commando attached. It would land immediately behind 2 E Yorks and wheel to the left to attack towards Ouistreham. The French commandos would then eliminate the casino strongpoint (WN-10) at Riva Bella, while 4 Commando attacked the gun battery on the beach at Ouistreham and cleared the town. Once these tasks were completed, 4 Commando would rejoin the main body of 1st Special Service Brigade. Lovat's second task was to make a speedy advance inland with the bulk of his brigade to the two bridges over the River Orne and its canal at Bénouville. Here they would link up with Maj-Gen Richard Gale's 6th Airborne Division, which would have landed during the night on the eastern side of the river.

Strongpoint Trout at the western end of Lion-sur-Mer, the D-Day target of 41 RM Commando. The house arrowed and the villa to the right of it can still be seen at the top of the beach. (*Private Collection/Archives du Mémorial de Caen*)

On the right flank of the landings, coming ashore immediately after 1 S Lancs on Queen White Beach, would be No. 41 (Royal Marine) Commando, from 4th Special Service Brigade. Its task was to move to the west and attack Lion-sur-Mer, clearing the seaside village and capturing the château and strongpoint WN-21 ('Trout'). The commando would then continue west to meet 48 RM Commando advancing from the Canadian landings on Juno, thus linking I Corps' two landing beaches.

The offensive to liberate Europe began in the first few minutes of 6 June 1944, when three Allied airborne divisions started descending onto Normandy. In the west, US 82nd and 101st Airborne Divisions landed to seize ground inland from Utah Beach. At the same time, Maj-Gen Gale brought his British 6th Airborne Division down into the area to the east of the River Orne. The division captured intact the bridges over the Orne and the adjacent canal at Bénouville, which provided the means of linking the airborne bridgehead to the landings on Sword, and carved out a bridgehead several kilometres deep. Gale then had to hold his gains and keep the Germans from attacking the seaborne landings from the east until relieved by the infantry and commandos landing with 3rd Infantry Division.

The descent of the paratroopers into the sector manned by 716th Infantry Division caused consternation to GenLt Richter. At 0110 hours he put his men on full alert. Throughout the remainder of the night more and more information came in to Richter's headquarters convincing him that a full-scale airborne landing was taking place in his sector. He contacted the headquarters of 21st Panzer Division and asked GenMaj Feuchtinger to send his entire division against the British paratroopers. Feuchtinger hesitated, for although there were standing orders for him to commit his division in the event of landings in 716th Division's sector, his division was part of Army Group B's armoured reserve and he needed higher confirmation regarding the best course of action. Were the landings just a raid, or were they a precursor to something bigger? Orders, however, were slow in coming, for the one man who would have made the right decision, Field Marshal Rommel, was away in Germany visiting his wife. By the time that 21st Panzer Division started to move against the airborne bridgehead it was getting light.

The invasion armada arrived off the coast of Normandy during darkness in the early hours of 6 June. The infantry of British 3rd Infantry Division were carried over the Channel in Landing Ships Infantry (LSI). Hanging from their davits were the assault landing craft (LCA) that would take the troops to the beaches. It took some time to load and lower these small boats

and to line up them in the water ready for their run to the shore. While this was proceeding, as dawn broke through an overcast sky, the softening-up process had begun on the shore defences. Allied bombers droned up and down the coastline showering known positions with high explosives. The bombardment was then taken up by the heavy guns of the battleships, monitors and cruisers. HMS *Warspite*, *Ramillies* and *Roberts* pounded the long-range coastal guns at Villerville, Benerville and Houlgate on the far side of the Orne with their 15-inch weapons. Closer to the beaches, the cruisers *Danae*, *Dragon*, and *Frobisher* attacked the gun batteries around Sword.

At 0600 hours, the flotillas of LCAs left the protection of their landing ships and headed for shore, joining with the other craft that made up the assault wave. Ahead of them were the tank landing craft (LCTs) carrying the DD Shermans of the 13th/18th Hussars. These larger vessels hove to 5,000 metres out from the beaches and swung round to bring their bows downwind so as to launch their vulnerable loads. The swimming tanks then gently eased their way down the ramps and into the choppy sea. Of the 40 DD tanks on board the LCTs, 34 were successfully launched and only two of these subsequently succumbed to the rough sea and sank. The others made it safely to the shore and emerged from the surf with the leading waves of infantry as planned.

A lone tourist walks along the beach near la Brèche, opposite the site of strong-point Cod at the junction of Queen Red and White sectors. On D-Day this was the landing point of the two assault battalions and their tank support. *(Author)*

Naval Bombardment of Sword Beach defences

Ship	Main armament	Target
HMS *Danae* (cruiser)	6 x 6-in	155-mm battery Daimler
Dragon (Polish cruiser)	6 x 6-in	100-mm battery Morris
HMS *Frobisher* (cruiser)	7 x 7.5-in	155-mm Ouistreham/ Riva Bella battery
HMS *Virago* (destroyer)	4 x 4.7-in	Lion-sur-Mer strongpoint Trout
HMS *Verulam* (destroyer)	4 x 4.7-in	Lion-sur-Mer beach defences
HMS *Serapis* (destroyer)	4 x 4.7-in	Queen White beach defences
HMS *Scourge* (destroyer)	4 x 4.7-in	Queen Red beach defences
Stord (Norwegian destroyer)	4 x 4.7-in	Ouistreham/Riva Bella beach defences
HMS *Scorpion* (destroyer)	8 x 4.7-in	Ouistreham/Riva Bella beach defences
HMS *Middleton* (destroyer)	6 x 4-in	Queen Red and White close beach defences in support of AVREs and LCTs
Slazak (Polish destroyer)	6 x 4-in	Queen Red and White close beach defences in support of AVREs and LCTs
HMS *Saumarez* (destroyer)	4 x 4.7-in	mouth of the Orne beach defences

The LCAs of the assault waves now began their run-in to the beaches. On either beam LCT(R)s sent salvoes of 5-inch rockets to pound the rear of the landing zone. LCGs, tank landing craft armed with 4.7-inch guns, also bombarded individual German positions from their open decks, as did the anti-aircraft guns on board the flak landing craft, LCT(F). This fire was taken up by the division's own self-propelled guns and by the 95-mm guns of the Centaur tanks manned by the Royal Marines in their LCT(A)s. Further out to sea, nine navy destroyers trained their guns on individual enemy strongpoints and opened fire. Beneath this hail of high explosive, the coastline disappeared behind palls of black smoke and sheets of yellow flame.

The heavy bombardment had obviously alerted the Germans to the landings and they now retaliated with artillery fire from their field and coastal batteries. Fountains of water were thrown up around the landing craft as the shells plunged down amongst them. Several of the LCTs took evasive action to avoid the fire, colliding with and sinking one of the DD tanks. At 0725 hours, H-Hour, the leading craft hit the shore, weaving their way in amongst the beach obstacles. Ramps went down and out came the infantry, charging their way up the sands and trying to ignore the small arms fire cracking through the air. With troops now on the beach, the run-in shoot by the artillery was complete and the

Aerial view, taken on 3 June, of the western part of strongpoint Cod, showing the maze of zig-zag trenches that linked the main positions of the fortification. 2 E Yorks landed immediately opposite this point near the junction of Queen Red and White Beaches. *(Keele Photo Library)*

LCTs carrying them turned away to wait the appointed time when they were programmed to land. Arriving on the beach with the infantry, instead of ahead of them as planned because of the rough sea, were the DD Shermans of the 13th/18th Hussars. The leading DD tanks touched down on the empty sands alongside the infantry much to the surprise of the German defenders. It took just one minute for each tank crew to drop the flotation screen, disengage the propulsion screw and convert the amphibious monster into a normal fighting tank with its 75-mm gun blazing away at the enemy. Moments later, amongst the swimming tanks and the infantry, came the LCTs carrying the flails, AVREs and armoured bulldozers of the 22nd Dragoons and 5th Assault Regiment, RE, of 79th Armoured Division.

Anti-tank gun emplacement at the top of the beach. This gun is probably the 50-mm weapon located on the eastern edge of strongpoint Cod. *(IWM B6379)*

Manning the defences along Queen Red and White Beaches was *Hauptmann* (Captain) Heinrich Kuhtz's 10th Company (of 3rd Battalion), 736th Grenadier Regiment. The defenders were well dug in, forming clusters around concrete gun pits, belts of wire and zig-zag lines of trenches. Anchoring these beach defences along Queen Beach was the large strongpoint WN-20 ('Cod') which covered an area roughly 350 metres wide from the small road running along the top of the beach to the larger lateral road some 150 metres inland. The strongpoint's firepower was made up of one 88-mm gun, three 50-mm anti-tank guns, three heavy mortars and six machine guns. Its guns covered the whole of the beach and they linked in with other positions further down each side of the shoreline.

To the east, on the edge of Queen Red, was a smaller strongpoint, WN-18, which housed a large casemate containing a 75-mm gun positioned to fire down the length of the shoreline, as well as a 50-mm anti-tank gun. To the west, the bricked-up seafront houses of Lion and concrete pill-boxes strung along the shore formed a continuous defensive link with WN-21 (Trout), where there was a 75-mm and another two 50-mm guns.

Landing craft bound for Sword Beach pass close by the headquarters ship of Assault Force S, HMS *Largs*. In the foreground, a tank landing craft has DD Shermans of 13th/18th Hussars on board. Across the middle of the picture, a line of infantry assault landing craft begin their run to the beaches carrying troops from the assault companies of 8th Infantry Brigade. *(IWM A23846)*

Strongpoint Cod was situated right on the boundary of White and Red Beaches immediately in front of the assaulting troops. Its capture was the first objective of A and B Companies of 2 E Yorks, landing on Queen Red. When the Yorkshiremen stormed out of their landing craft they ran directly into its line of fire. The defenders had taken shelter in deep concrete bunkers during the bombardment and now emerged to man their weapons and deal with the invaders. Machine-gun, mortar and rifle fire now poured out of strongpoint Cod. Most of it came straight at the two assault companies of 2 E Yorks, but the men of 1 S Lancs just to their right also felt the fury of this fire, losing A Company's OC, Major J.F. Harward, almost immediately.

The infantrymen knew that safety lay at the top of the beach under the guns, rather than on the exposed sands. Each of them now made a dash for cover and to get to grips with the enemy. Fire on the beach was deadly; machine-guns swept the sand and the anti-tank guns of the strongpoint were causing many problems to the armour. The tanks of 79th Armoured Division suffered particularly badly, especially those immediately in front of the guns on Queen Red. All of the breaching teams had tanks knocked out at almost point-blank range as they attempted to flail paths up to the dunes and lay bridges across the gaps to create exits from the beach. One LCT had a Crab tank disabled on its ramp, blocking further disembarkation. The resulting fire set ammunition alight and Lieutenant-Colonel (Lt-Col) A.D.B. Cocks, RE, overall commander of the beach clearing and gapping teams, was killed. Further west, on Queen White Beach, German fire was less intense and progress was made by the AVREs and flail tanks, so that a lane was quickly cleared and an exit made. Elsewhere, all immediate attempts to open lanes inland failed.

The men of 3rd Infantry Division were soon amongst the wire trying to force a way off the beach. On Queen White A and B Companies of 2 E Yorks found their progress completely blocked by Cod. The Yorkshiremen tried to get into the strongpoint, assisted by the tanks of 13th/18th Hussars, but there were too many weapons firing from too many angles to find a blind spot through which they could close on the fortifications. C Company from 1 S Lancs moved across to join in the assault on Cod, followed shortly afterwards by the remaining companies of the battalion as they came ashore. These follow-up waves of Lancashiremen landed further to the east than planned and came in under the active guns of strongpoint Cod. A number were killed the moment they tried to get off their landing craft. B Company lost its commander, Major R.H. Harrison, almost immediately, and then his replacement, Captain R.C. Bell-Walker, a few moments later. The death toll was rising rapidly. The next officer to fall was the battalion commander, Lt-Col R.P.H. Burbury. He was killed by a sniper soon after he left his assault craft.

The arrival of the extra troops and the perseverance of a few tank commanders gradually blasted aside the opposition

Main picture: Wire defences at the top of the beach between strongpoints WN-18 and WN-20 were easily breached, but were often backed up on their landward sides by minefields. In the background commandos from 1st Special Service Brigade are coming ashore from the infantry landing craft which brought them over the Channel. *(IWM B5270)*

Inset below: Lord Lovat brings his commandos ashore onto Queen Red Beach. The brigadier is the figure in the water to the left of the shoulder of the commando in the foreground, who is in fact Lovat's piper, Bill Millin. *(IWM B5103)*

defending strongpoint Cod. Troops worked their way down both sides of the fortified site and attempted an entry from the rear while the tanks fired high explosive rounds against the bunkers. Once a breach had been made through the wire and the mines, the infantry were soon amongst the trenches and pill-boxes, winkling out the defenders with rifle, grenade and bayonet. Gradually, one by one, the guns and mortars of Cod fell silent and the men of 8th Infantry Brigade started to look for ways off the beach towards their next objective.

The ground immediately to the south of the inland lateral road behind Red and White Beaches had been flooded and formed soft marshland. It forced the advance inland to be confined mostly to the lanes leading to Colleville and Hermanville. Both routes had mined verges, so there was little room for armour to deploy off these roads. 1 S Lancs swung to the right and began clearing the houses and villas along the beach, working westwards and onto the lateral road. 2 E Yorks did the same to the left, clearing opposition from the top of the beach and filtering through the houses and gardens to the east–west highway behind them.

DD Sherman tanks of B Squadron, 13th/18th Hussars, and infantry of 2 E Yorks moving along the lateral road towards Ouistreham. *(IWM MH2013)*

By this time the next phase of the landing was coming ashore, arriving between H+30 minutes and H+75. Included in these new arrivals were advance parties of the units which would begin to bring some order out of the chaos on the beach. Over the next few hours, sandwiched between new waves of infantry, armour and support vehicles, were men and equipment from 101st Beach Group Sub-Area including local defence infantry, engineers, signallers, medical groups, ordnance parties, provost companies and pioneers. These were the men who cleared obstacles, organised routes, directed traffic, dealt with casualties and generally kept things moving on and off the beach.

On each flank of Red and White Beaches it now became the turn of the commandos. At 0820 hours, 4 Commando, with its complement of Frenchmen led by *Commandant* (Captain) Philippe Kieffer, set down on Red Beach. They landed under heavy fire and had to fight their way up the beach into a belt of wire and mines. They also had to contend with the defences of strongpoint WN-18 at very close quarters. The commandos eventually forced an exit through the site of a pre-war holiday

Men from 4 Commando moving along the narrow-gauge railway behind the beach towards Ouistreham, on their way to attack the battery there. *(IWM BU1187)*

park and some seaside villas towards the road at the rear. This lateral road, which had a narrow-gauge railway line running alongside it, was about 200 metres inland and it formed the line of advance towards Ouistreham. Joining with the commandos were some of the men of 2 E Yorks who were also making their way eastwards on their way to strongpoint Sole. No. 4 Commando's objectives were the gun battery on the beach at Ouistreham and the casino strongpoint at Riva Bella; this latter resistance post was the particular target of Captain Kieffer's men.

At the same time, to the west on White Beach, the men of 41 RM Commando landed 300 metres to the left of their proposed site, actually coming ashore on Red Beach. Casualties were heavy from the fire of the still active strongpoint Cod. Once off the deadly shoreline, the men moved onto the lateral road and turned right to advance to their forming-up point near the road leading to Hermanville. Here they were organised into two groups: one attacking the château at Lion-sur-Mer and the other making for strongpoint Trout at the far end of the seaside village.

At 0840 hours Brigadier Lord Lovat arrived with 1st Special Service Brigade headquarters and 6 Commando, followed by 3 Commando and 45 RM Commando in successive waves. There was some fighting to be done before Lovat's men were off the beach for the Germans in WN-18 were still lively. Lovat's men made for the lateral road, storming several pill-boxes with grenade and Tommy gun as they went. The brigadier then took his men south into open country, heading for the airborne division's lodgement over the Orne, some 9 km away. With 6 Commando in the lead, they advanced along the route Colleville–St-Aubin-d'Arquenay–le Port–Bénouville. Their progress was heartened by news that Gale's paratroops had captured the bridges at Bénouville during the early hours. These isolated troops were, however, under attack by German panzergrenadiers and urgently needed support from the commandos.

The follow-up battalion of 8th Infantry Brigade, 1 Suffolks, came ashore at H+60 in the face of continued resistance. Most of the Germans in the immediate area had by that time been cleared, but sniper and mortar fire from still untaken positions inland remained a problem, as did longer-range shell fire from very active field batteries several kilometres behind the beach. 1 Suffolks landed with few casualties and managed to get off the beach and make their way to the rendezvous area in a wood a

The canal bridge at Bénouville captured in a brilliant *coup de main* by Major Howard's D Company, 2nd Oxford and Bucks Light Infantry, during the first few minutes of 6 June. The bridge was the main link between 6th Airborne Division's lodgement and the landings on Sword Beach. Howard's men landed just a few metres away by gliders and these can be seen in the background. (IWM B5288)

few hundred metres inland. Meanwhile, flail tanks swept minefields, and bridging tanks spanned anti-tank traps and ditches, allowing some of the armour also to get away from the chaos that was developing on the beach. An hour and a half after the first waves had hit the shore, the self-propelled guns of the division's field regiments were also landed. It was now mid-morning and getting towards high tide and the onshore wind had driven the sea up higher still until there was only about ten metres of dry sand at the top of the beach instead of the expected 30 metres. This narrow strip was gradually filling with tanks, bulldozers, jeeps, tracked carriers and infantry all seeking exits from the shoreline. Soon chaos ruled and Queen Beach was paralysed by a gigantic traffic jam.

By this time 1 S Lancs was well inland and at 0900 hours had entered Hermanville and set up its battalion headquarters. 2 E Yorks was moving through the fields towards its next objective, strongpoint WN-14 (Sole), which contained the headquarters of 1st Battalion, 736th Grenadier Regiment. This resistance post consisted of several underground personnel bunkers and close defence positions. 2 E Yorks arrived at the strongpoint from across the fields under enemy observation and was shelled and mortared all the way. The battalion's attack on Sole should have been supported by heavy fire from warships, but the naval bombardment officer who was to have controlled this was missing. Fortunately, a few mobile guns from 76th Field Regiment were at hand and they gave supporting fire as the infantry put in their assault. The German position was taken by a set-piece attack and the area quickly consolidated by more and more men of 2 E Yorks arriving from the beach. While this was going on the battalion commander, Lt-Col C.F. Hutchinson, was making a reconnaissance of the next objective about a kilometre away, the German 155-mm gun battery at strongpoint WN-12 (Daimler). The colonel's group were in a carrier in a sunken lane leading up to the post when they were hit by mortar fire. The colonel was wounded and had to be evacuated.

The gun battery within WN-12 was surrounded by a large

minefield and guarded by a number of concrete defence posts. Daimler was taken by 2 E Yorks after another set-piece attack in the mid-afternoon, this time supported by both 76th Field Regiment and some tanks from the 13th/18th Hussars. In a very short time the infantry had breached the perimeter and were dealing with the garrison. The German defenders inside, from 4th Battery, 1716th Artillery Regiment, put up little resistance

A Tobruk weapons pit which once formed part of the outer defences of battery Daimler. *(Author)*

once an entry had been forced into the position and 70 of them quickly surrendered.

Behind 2 E Yorks in Ouistreham, 4 Commando was engaging its objectives from the rear. The commando had moved eastwards along the lateral road into the town with Captain Kieffer and his

Frenchmen having been given the honour of leading the way. Kieffer's men were given the task of capturing the casino strongpoint at Riva Bella. The pre-war casino building itself no longer existed because the Germans had demolished it and built a fortified position on top of its rubble. The resulting strongpoint included concrete bunkers, pill-boxes and individual Tobruk-pattern weapon pits linked together with field works and trenches. Again, like all other strongpoints, the surrounding area was mined and shielded by barbed wire entanglements. Concrete 'dragon's teeth' covered the seaward approaches and provided an anti-tank screen.

The modern casino at Riva Bella was built on the site of the pre-war building, demolished by the Germans. *(Author)*

The capture of this resistance post proved to be a difficult proposition for the lightly armed French commandos. They attacked it in two groups from the rear, but bravery and determination were not enough to affect a break-in. Fire from concealed positions, especially from a large bunker topped with a steel cupola, caused many casualties and these positions proved impossible to approach. A 50-mm anti-tank gun in a bunker and defenders in a large water tower overlooking the site also caused much discomfort. After half an hour of fighting Kieffer and his men were no nearer to capturing the casino position, and their numbers were rapidly diminishing. Then news came that some DD tanks had arrived in the streets to the rear and Kieffer left to seek their help. In a few moments he returned riding on the top of one of the Shermans and directed its fire against the positions that had given his men so much trouble. One by one high explosive shells fired at very short range disposed of them. Then a breach through the wire was made and the Frenchmen worked their way into the trenches and dug-outs at the heart of the strongpoint, clearing the disheartened enemy as they went. By late morning the casino strongpoint had been eliminated.

The war correspondent Chester Wilmot talks with some French commandos of 10 (Inter-Allied) Commando, after their successful attack on the casino position at Riva Bella. (IWM B5278)

Further to the east, the bulk of 4 Commando continued to close on the rear of the seafront gun battery close by the mouth of the River Orne. The commandos approached along the side streets of Ouistreham. They crossed the anti-tank ditch protecting the fortified area around the gun pits and soon made contact with the German defenders within the perimeter of minefields and wire surrounding the site. Overlooking the landward side, looking down on every approach, was a very large reinforced concrete tower, over 17 metres high with a wide observation slit

HISTORY

just below its roof. This housed the control and ranging observers for the coastal guns. It was not built as a fighting position and was only armed with a 20-mm anti-aircraft cannon on its roof and a few light machine guns inside. Nonetheless, the commanding position of these weapons still caused problems for the commandos, as did the shower of grenades thrown at them from the tower as they passed by underneath. The massive bunker itself presented an impregnable face to the commandos and they left its capture to follow-up troops, pressing on with their more immediate goal of eliminating the gun battery.

The fortifications and field works surrounding the gun site were attacked by 4 Commando in a series of rapid movements and bursts of fire. The commandos went at the defenders from a number of directions at the same time, never allowing the Germans holed up inside the battery to concentrate their fire in return. Using any available cover, the attackers fired as they ran, ducking into bomb craters and flopping down behind mounds in the sand. They blew gaps in the wire with Bangalore torpedoes and were soon amongst the trenches, sweeping them clear with Thompson sub-machine guns and grenades. When they approached the open artillery gun pits they found them to be empty. Rommel had in fact decided on 15 May, after visiting

Anti-tank ditch guarding the landward flank of the strongpoint at Ouistreham/Riva Bella. This obstacle had to be negotiated by 4 Commando during the attack on the gun site. (*Private Collection/Archives du Mémorial de Caen*)

Normandy and the Pas de Calais, to pull back all the guns in army coast batteries which were not protected by overhead concrete emplacements to sites inland, in view of their vulnerability to air attack.

With the threat of the guns now gone, it was pointless to continue with the attack. The remaining Germans in the position could be mopped up by the infantry who were now arriving in Ouistreham, so the commandos withdrew into the town to continue clearing its houses and to regroup to rejoin the rest

Sword Beach near the junction of Queen Red and White sectors opposite strongpoint Cod. In the foreground are two sappers from 101st Beach Group, recognisable from their white-banded steel helmets and anchor shoulder patches. Behind them men of 41 RM Commando are coming ashore. *(IWM B5114)*

of 1st Special Service Brigade on the opposite side of the River Orne.

The remainder of Lord Lovat's 1st Special Service Brigade had landed a little later than 4 Commando and had exited the beach near the road to Colleville, heading southwards towards that village. Once clear of the seafront the main body of the brigade found the opposition weak and sporadic. At times there was nothing more than the occasional sniper to harry the commandos on their way, but immediately they approached the buildings of the inland villages they found that the resistance was more organised. On the outskirts of Colleville two stubborn pill-boxes caused problems, but swift attacks by the lightly armed troops quickly captured them. They left the clearing of Colleville itself to the men of 1 Suffolks, who were arriving there as the commandos pressed on. St-Aubin-d'Arquenay was reached and cleared and a German column was attacked and eliminated on the outskirts of the village before the commandos moved on down the slope towards the Orne, with 6 Commando in the lead. On approaching le Port, the noise of the stubborn fire-fight put up by Gale's men could be heard as the paratroopers beat off yet

HISTORY

another attack. At Bénouville, the commandos joined up with the airborne troops and were cheered as they advanced down the slope to the bridge over the canal. The airborne assault and the seaborne landings had linked up. It was just after 1300 hours.

On the other (western) side of the landings on Queen Beach, 41 RM Commando was pressing into Lion-sur-Mer towards its objectives. The commando had been split into two groups for the attacks, with one, led by the battalion commander, clearing the town towards strongpoint Trout and the other, led by his second-in-command, moving on the château. When Lt-Col T.M. Gray gathered his men at their assembly point he found that his second group had been severely reduced by German fire and had lost its commander, a troop leader, the signals officer and regimental sergeant-major, all killed on the beach. Gray decided to press on with his mission as planned and moved his men into Lion-sur-Mer, establishing his headquarters in the town by the church. P and Y Troops continued through the village towards the strongpoint, to find that the Germans had virtually quit the built-up area, but were still holding Trout in some force. When the commandos approached closer to the strongpoint their advance was stopped by machine-gun and mortar fire. At around 1100 hours three AVREs came up the main road in support, trying to get close enough to launch an attack against the fortifications with their heavy mortars. Unfortunately, a 50-mm anti-tank gun got off the first shots and all three were knocked out. The other group of marines fought their way to the road junction near the château grounds when they, too, were stopped by German fire, both from Trout and from across the open country to the south.

A stalemate now developed, for both attacks needed the support of heavier weapons and none were forthcoming. Communications between the commando and the guns in the rear had been lost. Just after midday this inactivity was broken by a counter-attack into the commando's left flank. A Troop was hit by a group of about 60 Germans supported by mortars and self-propelled infantry guns. Lt-Col Gray recognised the vulnerability of his strung-out commando and withdrew all of his marines to a more easily defensible position around the church.

The German troops hitting 41 RM Commando, and the few men of 1 S Lancs who were in the area, were from GenLt Richter's 716th Infantry Division. For most of the time Richter's units were just struggling to survive against overwhelming odds.

Commandos, most likely from 41 RM Commando, wait for orders at the top of the beach. Such a concentration of men would have been incredibly vulnerable to the shell fire which plagued the landing sites until early afternoon. *(IWM B5090)*

Those who were protected inside concrete strongpoints fought well enough, but many of those in open emplacements and in field positions fell back as the British forces advanced. One group, accompanied by *Leutnant* (2nd Lieutenant) Rudolf Schaaf, did exactly the opposite and counter-attacked. Schaaf commanded 10th Battery, 1716th Artillery Regiment, and had his mobile 155-mm guns established on Périers Ridge near Plumetot, 3 km from the sea, when the landings began. From his position he could see the Allied armada disgorging vast quantities of men and equipment over the beaches at la Brèche. His guns opened fire, but soon lost their forward observer when his position in one of the resistance nests on the beach was captured. From then on Schaaf's guns had to fire on the established bearings and ranges of pre-determined targets, which had been calculated during the weeks before the invasion.

Towards the end of the morning, 10th Battery was ordered to take its guns and support a group of infantry from 3rd Battalion of Colonel Krug's 736th Grenadier Regiment in an attack towards Lion-sur-Mer in order to recapture the beach at la Brèche. The small battle group made its way down the hillside in open order and struck 41 RM Commando in its flank. The artillery fired into the buildings of Lion over open sights and tore into the lightly-armed British troops. For a while the attackers had the upper hand and German grenadiers moved into some of the outlying buildings and captured a few of the commandos and infantry. Then concentrated counter-fire was brought down on them, which began to force them back. Heavy shell fire from warships and artillery then joined in with the small arms fire of the commandos and the Germans retired back up the hill towards the top of the ridge. Schaaf managed to withdraw all of his guns intact and get them back into his original positions north of Plumetot. The brave but futile counter-attack, the only one made that day against Sword Beach by German 716th Infantry Division, had failed, but the threat it presented to the flanks of the British troops holding Lion caused 41 RM Commando to postpone its attacks on Trout and the château until the next day.

Medics deal with the dead and wounded in the shelter of an abandoned AVRE tank from 79th Armoured Division. To the right is an M10 Wolverine from 20th Anti-tank Regiment. *(IWM B5095)*

CHAPTER 4

EXPANDING THE BEACHHEAD

The follow-up landings over Sword Beach were complicated. After the initial assault waves had captured the landing site, a programme of introducing into the beachhead just the right amounts of supply and support that were necessary to maintain the momentum of the attack was implemented. Behind the men and guns of the assault brigade, came their priority vehicles and stores. The landing of these elements was planned to conclude by H+120 (0925 hours). Then the intermediate brigade landed between H+150 and H+250, that is between 0955 hours and 1135 hours. This was 185th Infantry Brigade, with 2 KSLI, 2 Warwicks and 1 Norfolks, together with the supporting armour of the Staffordshire Yeomanry and its priority vehicles and stores. After 185th Infantry Brigade it was the turn of 9th Infantry Brigade, the reserve brigade. This was expected to come ashore between H+270 and H+360 (1155 hours and 1335 hours), bringing with it 2 Lincs, 1 KOSB and 2 RUR, together with the last of 27th Armoured Brigade's regiments, the East Riding Yeomanry.

The Château d'Hermanville was used on 6 June as the headquarters of Maj-Gen Rennie's British 3rd Infantry Division. It is now the town's *mairie*. (*Author*)

Traffic jams beginning to build up along the lateral road behind the beach. This view is looking westwards towards the junction with the main road to Hermanville. The tall building in the top centre of the picture is the present-day hotel on the Place du Cuirassé Courbet. *(IWM B5084)*

By 1100 hours, the three battalions of 185th Infantry Brigade were ashore and in the brigade assembly area near Hermanville-sur-Mer, with 2 Warwicks on the right, 2 KSLI in the middle and 1 Norfolks on the left near Colleville. The brigade's main task that day, and that of 3rd Infantry Division, was the capture of Caen. Its commander, Brigadier K.P. Smith, had planned for a mobile group, led by 2 KSLI on the tanks of the Staffordshire Yeomanry, to advance along the direct route from Hermanville to Caen as quickly as possible. However, when his men were assembled and ready to move at 1100 hours, there was no sign of its supporting tanks. The Shermans of the Staffordshire Yeomanry were still stuck on the beach. The high tide had reduced the width of the beach to just a narrow strip and the sands were now covered in stalled armour and transport. Those vehicles that had got off the beach were congregating along the single lateral road at the rear. It was impossible to deploy off this

HISTORY

road because of the minefields and flooded ground to the south. Brigadier Smith was in something of a dilemma: should he wait for the tanks, or should he order 2 KSLI to start out for Caen on foot and send the tanks on when they arrived? He decided to wait, but then at midday, when the tanks had still not arrived, he ordered 2 KSLI to begin its advance along the main axis on foot.

In Colleville 1 Suffolks was clearing the village before undertaking its next objectives, the reduction of the strongpoints of Morris and Hillman and the move south to Périers Ridge. The Suffolks completed the task that had been started by Lovat's commandos on their way through to the bridges over the Orne at Bénouville and swept Colleville clear of the enemy. At 1230 hours B Company moved forward towards the 100-mm gun battery at Morris (2nd Battery, 1716th Artillery Regiment) and began its assault plan. First, the outer wire of the strongpoint would be blown with Bangalore torpedoes, then a barrage would be laid on the battery by the guns of 76th Field Regiment before the infantry rushed the concrete emplacements and defensive pill-boxes. The preparation proved to be unnecessary for, just before the wire was blown, a white flag was produced and the whole garrison of 67 Germans surrendered. The troops inside Morris had been bombed by aircraft and shelled by warships since before dawn; they clearly had no stomach for further fighting and shelling. It was 1300 hours and 1 Suffolks now moved on southwards out of Colleville to close on strongpoint Hillman.

Battery Morris, captured by 1 Suffolks on D-Day. Construction work on one of the casemates was in progress at the time of the invasion. (IWM B5878)

HISTORY

Then: A large party of British troops escorts two German prisoners back to the beach along the road from Hermanville. *(IWM B5027)*

Now: The road to Hermanville just inland from the exit from Queen White Beach. The half-timbered building remains almost as it was in June 1944. *(Author)*

General Marcks, commander of LXXXIV Corps, was finally given permission to deploy 21st Panzer Division during the late morning. He did not agree with GenLt Richter that the best use of the tanks was against the airborne lodgement to the east of the Orne and by this time Richter realised that the decision he had made in the early hours of the morning had been a mistake. It was clear that the main danger lay in the landings by British 3rd Infantry Division at la Brèche. Marcks now ordered Feuchtinger to concentrate his panzer division to the north of Caen and prepare to launch an attack against the landings. By the time this order was issued to the troops in the line, some units could not be disengaged from their battle with 6th Airborne Division, so most of 125th Panzergrenadier Regiment and 4th Company of 100th/22nd Panzer Regiment had to remain east of the Orne. The rest of 21st Panzer Division drove back into Caen, crossed the town bridges and moved north along the road to Douvres to deploy along the line Lébisey–Épron–St-Contest, harassed all the way by naval gunfire and aerial bombing. At 1500 hours, Hitler's HQ had decided to release the panzer reserves. Marcks was told

Colonel Hermann von Oppeln-Bronikowski, commander of 100th/22nd Panzer Regiment. His tanks led the counter-attack on the afternoon of 6 June. He was promoted to command 24th Panzer Division in October 1944. (*Bundesarchiv 101/721/376/6A*)

that the *Hitlerjugend* Division had also been subordinated to his LXXXIV Corps, but as it was still in the process of moving to the Caen area, it would not arrive in time to take part in the counter-attack. Marcks could not afford to wait for it to arrive.

Feuchtinger's division was formed into two groups. The first, commanded by *Oberst* (Colonel) Hermann von Oppeln-Bronikowski, consisted of both tank battalions of 100th/22nd Panzer Regiment (less 4th Company); 1st Battalion, 125th Panzergrenadier Regiment; 1st Company, 220th Panzer Pioneer Battalion; and 3rd Battalion, 155th Panzer Artillery Regiment. Its objective was the landing beach at la Brèche.

HISTORY

A section of Queen White Beach at la Brèche. Transport is off the beach and moving along the lateral road to the rear (now the D514). *(IWM CL25)*

The other column was commanded by *Oberst* Rauch and contained 1st Battalion of Rauch's 192nd Panzergrenadier Regiment; 2nd Company, 220th Panzer Pioneer Battalion; and 2nd Battalion, 155th Panzer Artillery Regiment. Its target was the still-uncaptured shoreline between Lion and Luc-sur-Mer. The two groups were told to pass on either side of Point 61 on Périers Ridge (Point 58 on modern maps). Once they had reached the sea they would turn along the coast and roll up the landings.

By 1530 hours the division was in position and ready to attack. General Marcks came forward to Lébisey to watch the assembly. He knew that this attack was the most important move his corps would make that day. Marcks visited Colonel von Oppeln at his regimental command post and said to him: 'Oppeln, if you don't succeed in throwing the British into the sea we shall have lost the war.' Victory or defeat rested on the 98 tanks of Oppeln's panzer regiment.

While Marcks was assembling these panzer units, the British 185th Infantry Brigade's drive on Caen was passing within sight of Hillman, advancing out of Hermanville on foot up the northern slopes of Périers Ridge towards the crossroads at Point 61. In support were the guns of 7th and 33rd Field Regiments, controlled by forward observation officers up with the leading troops. Also on call were the self-propelled M10 guns of 41st

Anti-tank Battery and two troops of flail tanks from A Squadron, Westminster Dragoons. When the leading company of 2 KSLI had reached the top of the rise near Point 61, it was joined by the tanks of the first two squadrons of the Staffordshire Yeomanry who had managed to get clear of the beach and catch up. C Squadron was sent on with the infantry on the road, while B Squadron protected the right flank of the advance. Progress all the way up the slopes of Périers Ridge had been dogged by German mortar and small arms fire. Once the leading group had crested the rise and begun its descent towards Beuville, this fire was taken up by a 105-mm battery near Périers-sur-le-Dan. Then an 88-mm gun opened fire on B Squadron and knocked out five of the Staffordshire Yeomanry's tanks.

By this time the ridge should have been taken by 1 Suffolks, but that battalion was still over 1.5 km behind in Colleville, dealing with Morris and Hillman. The gunfire aimed at the KSLI advance was coming from a field position that was covered by wire and defensive outposts. The battery had been attacked that morning by the RAF during the pre-invasion bombing, but it was obviously still full of fight. Lt-Col F.J. Maurice, commander of 2 KSLI, detached a company to deal with the artillery. After a prolonged and difficult fire-fight at very close range, Z Company managed to enter the battery and destroy the guns, capturing a few of the enemy inside in the process. Most of the defenders took flight just before the final attack. It was 1430 hours before the advance could continue.

Lt-Col Maurice led his men down the south slopes of Périers Ridge towards the long straggling village of Beuville into a good deal of rifle and machine-gun fire from its houses. He decided to leapfrog this resistance with Y and W Companies by moving them through the open ground to the right, while he sent the tanks and the rest of the infantry through the village. Then, to protect his right flank from the open country alongside of his advance, Lt-Col Maurice ordered 41st Anti-tank Battery to line its guns along the southern face of Périers Ridge and brought his own 6-pounder anti-tank guns to the western outskirts of Beuville. B Squadron of the Staffordshire Yeomanry had also been left hull-down further up Périers Ridge, helping to anchor this vulnerable south-western face of the advance.

Beuville was successfully captured without incident, but there was a great deal of resistance in the next village of Biéville,

M10 Wolverine 'tank buster' from 20th Anti-tank Regiment gives supporting fire to men from 2 E Yorks. *(IWM B5088)*

centred upon its château. W Company lost its commander and another officer there before the area was cleared. These moves took most of the afternoon and it was 1600 hours before the leading troops and tanks reached the southern end of Biéville. Ahead of them, the road to Caen dipped down to cross a steep-sided valley, which formed a natural anti-tank ditch. On the other side of this feature the road led up to a long tree-covered ridge. To the right of the road was the village of Lébisey; to the left were the Lébisey Woods. At 1625 hours, just as the battalion was preparing to move towards Lébisey, tanks were seen approaching from the south-west towards the right flank of 2 KSLI. GenMaj Feuchtinger had at last launched his counter-attack.

In Colleville earlier that afternoon, 1 Suffolks had opened its attack on Hillman. The great strongpoint which housed Colonel Krug's regimental headquarters covered an area 550 metres by 350 metres and contained two large H605-type bunkers topped by steel cupolas, as well as numerous other subterranean shelters, Tobruk emplacements, trenches and infantry guns covering every approach. Surrounding the site were two wire entanglements separated by an extensive minefield. At 1310 hours, the attack began with a barrage of high explosive fired by the guns of 7th Field Regiment and the battalion's own 3-inch mortars. Under this bombardment the men of the breaching platoon moved forward close to the outer wire. When they were ready to start their work the artillery switched to smoke. A gap in the wire was blown with Bangalore torpedoes and then mine-clearing parties moved up to clear and mark a lane through the minefield. Next, the inner wire was breached and A Company launched its assault.

The men of the leading platoon got through the breach and amongst the trenches of the strongpoint, but were quickly stopped by the volume of fire coming from the concrete shelters. Heavy machine guns swept the inside of Hillman from close range. The defenders also had the gap covered and any new attempt to get more men through it resulted in further casualties. Smoke was put down to try to conceal the entry of the next platoon and its men came forward to brave the fire. Only four men (Captain R. Ryley – the company commander, Lieutenants T. Tooley and J. Powell, and Corporal F. Stares) got through into the German trench system. Then they, too, were brought to a standstill by the machine guns. Stares, Tooley and Ryley were killed; it proved to be impossible to move across the open area inside Hillman.

A jumble of men and machines, including beach group personnel, take shelter from German fire on Sword Beach during the morning of 6 June. *(IWM B5093)*

Lt-Col R.E. Goodwin (CO 1 Suffolks) now decided to bring tanks forward to the edge of the outer wire to give his infantry close support. A troop of Shermans from C Squadron, 13th/18th Hussars, came up the sunken lane from the village and started firing high explosive into the compound. Their shells had little effect, for almost the whole of Hillman was underground and the tank fire could not penetrate the concrete emplacements. The

German field works and defences at Colleville, as plotted by British Intelligence. The two prominent features in blue on the map are the defences surrounding battery Morris (*nearest Colleville*) and the headquarters of 736th Grenadier Regiment at Hillman. The R15 is the road from Hermanville onto the Périers Ridge. *(Base map: GSGS 4347 Ouistreham 40/16NW, Stop Press edition, 20 May 1944)*

The ground inside strongpoint Hillman. The steel cupola and the concrete strip in the foreground are the only parts of Colonel Krug's command post that were visible above ground. The breach made by 1 Suffolks through the wire and minefields was located in the right background near the line of trees. *(Author)*

only prominent features of the strongpoint that were visible were the armoured steel cupolas on top of the bunkers and these, and the machine guns inside, were impervious to shot and shell. Goodwin ordered a larger gap to be blown in the wire and minefields to allow the tanks into the fortified area. It was really a task for a flail tank, but none were available. However, when a sapper officer, Lieutenant Arthur Heal, investigated the minefield he found that they were old British Mark III mines buried in four rows at 5-metre intervals. Heal decided to link the mines together with fuses and gelignite and then blew the lot. The resulting explosion cleared a gap large enough for tanks to pass through.

The delay in capturing Hillman was causing problems for everyone involved in the advance on Caen, for Périers Ridge was still not occupied and the ground south of Colleville was still swept by German fire. In the mid-afternoon the commander of 3rd Infantry Division, Maj-Gen Rennie, came forward to Colleville to meet with Lt-Col Goodwin to see how the reduction of Hillman was getting on. Goodwin explained the situation and was told that the strongpoint had to be taken by nightfall and 1 Suffolks dug in on the position ready to deal with German armour, which would be likely to mount an attack before dawn. Goodwin assured him that 1 Suffolks would succeed.

By this time 2 KSLI's advance on Caen was well underway and Brigadier Smith had brought the other two battalions of 185th

Infantry Brigade, 1 Norfolks and 2 Warwicks, across behind 1 Suffolks in Colleville. These two battalions should have been following along the main route of 2 KSLI, but the German resistance on Périers Ridge had forced Smith to send them round Colleville onto the left of the advance. 2 Warwicks was ordered to move through St-Aubin-d'Arquenay to support the paratroopers at Bénouville and to push forward towards Caen up the western side of the Orne canal, on the left flank of the armoured column of 2 KSLI.

The ground over which 1 Norfolks advanced towards Rover, seen from the roof of one of the bunkers within Hillman. *(Author)*

1 Norfolks had as its first objective the hilltop farm of Bellevue, code-named 'Rover', just to the east of Beuville, but could not advance out of Colleville until Hillman was captured. 1 Norfolks waited for two and half hours for the strongpoint to be taken and then the CO decided that he had to press on with the advance regardless. Two companies moved out into the open across the fields to the east of Hillman and were devastated by fire from the besieged fortification, losing 14 killed and many more wounded. The rest of the battalion tried to move further to the left and fared a little better by passing through St-Aubin-d'Arquenay. However, it was early evening before 1 Norfolks had completed its attack and established itself on Rover. Here the advance halted and the battalion dug in for the night.

Earlier that afternoon, just to the south of these positions, from the hillside above the advance units of 2 KSLI's armoured

A German tank crew take refreshment in a village near their concentration area at St-Pierre-sur-Dives. The tank is an early Panzer IV Model C, with a short barrelled 75-mm gun, from 100th/22nd Panzer Regiment of 21st Panzer Division. The division was armed with many of these obsolete machines and some old French Somua tanks at the time of the landings. (*Bundesarchiv 101/721/378/33*)

column, Feuchtinger's division had launched its attack. The tanks that swept northwards from the hill on their drive to the sea were from *Major* Vierzig's 2nd Battalion, 100th/22nd Panzer Regiment. They came down the slopes from the woods near Lébisey and drove across the right side of 185th Infantry Brigade's positions. C Squadron, Staffordshire Yeomanry, which had by now come forward to join 2 KSLI, opened fire immediately and hit one of the panzers. Then the anti-tank guns screening this western side of the brigade joined in. The fire hit more tanks and forced the German armour further over to the west where they ran broadside on to the guns of the Staffordshire Yeomanry's A Squadron. The shock of finding his battalion caught in the flanks by such ferocious anti-tank fire caused Vierzig to call for the attack to be broken off.

Major von Gottberg's 1st Battalion, 100th/22nd Panzer Regiment, was, however, out of range of this fire, for it had launched its attack further to the west. Its panzers left the area of Cambes/ Épron, passed on either side of the Château de la Londe, and then skirted round the eastern side of Mathieu. When it began to crest Périers Ridge, the battalion was hit by the anti-tank guns of 41st Anti-tank Regiment and the Sherman Fireflies of the Staffordshire Yeomanry's B Squadron which held the heights around Point 61. Six tanks were knocked out and many others were damaged. Von Gottberg tried to swing his battalion even further to the west and took it behind Périers-sur-le-Dan, but when its tanks again reached the crest on the western side of Périers, the results were the same; three more were destroyed. This second attack was then broken off. Feuchtinger's division had lost 14 tanks destroyed and over 50 damaged in all.

Order of Battle: 27th Armoured Brigade 6 JUNE 1944

The brigade contained a brigade headquarters and three armoured regiments:

13th/18th Royal Hussars
1st East Riding Yeomanry
The Staffordshire Yeomanry

The brigade was originally formed in 1940 from 1st Armoured Reconnaissance Brigade and spent the next four years training in England. For the first two years it was part of 9th Armoured Division before joining I Corps as an independent armoured brigade. It was disbanded in July 1944.

Each of the regiments was composed of three tank squadrons – A, B and C – and one Regimental HQ Squadron. HQ Squadron comprised 1 troop of 4 Sherman tanks for local protection; 1 anti-aircraft troop of 6 Crusader tanks, each mounting twin 20-mm Oerlikon guns; 1 reconnaissance troop of 11 light Stuart tanks each armed with a 37-mm gun; 1 liaison platoon of 9 scout cars; and 1 administration platoon of ambulances, trucks, jeeps and motorbikes for medical, messing, transport and workshop functions.

Each tank squadron had 5 troops of 3 Sherman tanks, plus 2 normal gun Shermans and a recovery Sherman in the squadron headquarters. In each troop, 2 of the tanks had the standard 75-mm gun, while the third had the more powerful 17-pounder gun giving it a firepower that almost equalled that of the German Panthers and Tigers. At full strength the regiment fielded 72 gun tanks and 60 other vehicles.

The other of GenMaj Feuchtinger's battle groups from 21st Panzer Division, that led by Colonel Rauch, launched its attack from the area of St-Contest, 3 km to the west of von Oppeln's start line. Its path northwards passed through the gap between British 3rd Infantry Division and Canadian 3rd Infantry Division (from Juno Beach), taking it just east of Mathieu and west of Cresserons. It came under long range fire from the guns of 185th Infantry Brigade near Point 61 and those on the ridge, but its leading elements actually made it to the sea between Luc-sur-Mer and Lion-sur-Mer in the early evening. Here they met up with the German troops still holding the adjacent seaside villages and from strongpoint Trout. Preparations were made to exploit this advance, but events later that evening made this impossible.

Brigadier Cunningham's 9th Infantry Brigade had started its landings in the late morning and had moved to its assembly area between Hermanville and Lion-sur-Mer without any major losses or incidents, ready to begin its advance to seize the ground between 185th Infantry Brigade and 9th Canadian Infantry Brigade. Just after 1300 hours, the personnel of the brigade

Brigadier E. Prior-Palmer, commander of 27th Armoured Brigade, sitting on the roof of his armoured car, gives orders to his staff captain during the advance inland. *(IWM B5022)*

headquarters landed and set up a field position close to Lion-sur-Mer. It was almost immediately hit by a mortar bomb, which killed and wounded many of the staff, including Brigadier Cunningham. Lt-Col A.D.G. Orr, the second-in-command, was away at the time liaising with Maj-Gen Gale in 6th Airborne Division's bridgehead. For a while, co-ordination of the brigade was lost until Orr joined up with the depleted headquarters.

Orr's taking charge of the brigade coincided with a change of plan. The threat against the airborne sector was seen as being most crucial and so Maj-Gen Rennie decided to move some of 9th Infantry Brigade's strength over from the right of the beachhead to the left. 1 KOSB was told to relieve the few men of 1 E Yorks who were holding St-Aubin-d'Arquenay and to secure the line overlooking the airborne lodgement across the river. By this time 9th Infantry Brigade's 2 Lincolns had become embroiled in fighting north of Cresserons and so that battalion was told to remain there. 2 RUR was moved to take up a position around Point 61. The attack by 21st Panzer Division had evidently caused some loss of nerve in the British camp; the priority now was to hold what had been taken, rather than seize new ground. It would appear that 9th Infantry Brigade's role in the rapid advance on Caen had been abandoned for one of consolidation.

Troops of 101st Beach Group dig in at the top of the beach in front of the large casemate of German strongpoint WN-18, near the junction of Queen and Roger sectors of Sword Beach. *(IWM B5180)*

At 1615 hours, just as the elements of 21st Panzer Division were launching their counter-attack from Lébisey, the tanks of 13th/18th Hussars started through the gap in Hillman's minefield, followed by the infantry. Once they were through the opening, the troops of 1 Suffolks fanned out along the trenches and attacked enemy positions. Machine-gun fire from the steel

HISTORY

cupolas still raked the open areas, but the tanks returned this fire allowing 1 Suffolks to close on the entrances to the casemates. There were few defenders left in the interlocking trenches between the concrete positions, most having withdrawn into the shelters. Each of these emplacements now had to be cleared by hand. The infantry stalked the bunkers, firing continuously on their weapon slits whilst pioneers crept forward to lay explosive charges at their entrances and drop grenades down ventilation shafts. One by one they blasted their way through steel doors and sprayed the insides with automatic fire, throwing grenades through any opening they came to. It was enough for most of the defenders and all resistance ended at around 2000 hours that evening. The rest of the night was spent mopping up the site while two of 1 Suffolks' companies moved 1 km southwards and captured the farm building of Beauvais to consolidate the battalion's hold on the area. This was not, however, the end of the Hillman operation, for the next morning, at 0645 hours, the last of the bunkers was opened and out walked Colonel Krug to surrender, together with two more officers and 70 other ranks.

Colonel Krug's command bunker at Hillman. The view is looking north-west towards Hermanville. Battery Morris is behind the trees on the right, beyond the electricity pylon. *(Author)*

In the late afternoon, 2 Warwicks, which had been waiting in Colleville to continue its move towards Caen, was told to move across to Bénouville and Blainville to prevent the Germans attacking down the road from Caen to Ouistreham. The battalion advanced out of Colleville through St-Aubin-d'Arquenay to the hamlet of le Port. Here it joined in the struggle in support of the paratroopers at Bénouville and came under a great deal of fire from troops of 21st Panzer Division. 2 Warwicks was attacked by infantry and a mobile 88-mm gun from 125th Panzergrenadier Regiment, which had remained by the Orne in contact with the airborne troops. It took all the afternoon and evening to complete this move and it was not until 2000 hours that the battalion could relieve the besieged 7th Battalion, The Parachute Regiment, of the responsibility of holding Bénouville and the bridges. By darkness, forward elements of the battalion had pushed the panzergrenadiers back up the Orne valley and arrived on the outskirts of Blainville where they dug in for the night.

After blunting the counter-attack of 21st Panzer Division, Lt-Col Maurice continued with his battalion's advance. He had halted the forward elements of 2 KSLI short of the natural anti-tank ditch south of Biéville and he now decided to push Y Company, led by Major P.C. Steele, forward across the ditch and up into the woods by Lébisey. By 1730 hours, Steele and his men had successfully negotiated the steep valley and reached the northern outskirts of Lébisey itself. Here they were held up by machine-gun fire and it soon became obvious that the Germans were in the village in some strength. A party of over 40 were seen trying to move round the right flank into the anti-tank ditch to get behind Y Company. Steele called for reinforcements to join his exposed company but Lt-Col Maurice decided that it was beyond the power of his strung-out column to take Lébisey that evening. The German attack had slowed his thrust on Caen and he now felt too exposed to continue. Both flanks were open, for 1 Norfolks was only just reaching Rover some 3 km back and the nearest friendly troops on the right were nearly 5 km away, south of Hermanville. Maurice therefore sent orders for Y Company to pull back into Biéville after dark and told his battalion to dig in for the night. Caen was not to be reached that day.

At around 2100 hours, the attention of all the troops in the area turned skywards towards the dull roar of hundreds of aircraft. The sky was full of planes and gliders sweeping low over the battlefield. On the flat landing ground to the south-east of St-Aubin-d'Arquenay, designated Landing Zone W (LZ W), and on LZ N near Ranville on the eastern side of the Orne, the follow-up

Men of 3rd Infantry Division watch the airborne resupply of Maj-Gen Gale's paratroopers on the evening of 6 June. *(IWM B5046)*

troops of 6th Airborne Division began to land. 6th Airlanding Brigade arrived in a fleet of 248 gliders, giving the troops on the ground the most impressive display of air power they had ever seen. Then came another 50 Dakota aircraft releasing hundreds of parachutes carrying the 116 tons of supplies to be delivered to Gale's men by air. No one who witnessed the event failed to be impressed by the dramatic arrival of these reinforcements.

The fly-in caused consternation in the German camp. Colonel Rauch, with his panzergrenadiers on the seafront between Lion and Luc-sur-Mer, was appalled by the scene. The massed descent of a whole airborne brigade, apparently in his rear, made his position untenable. There was also no means of interfering with the landings; no *Luftwaffe* aircraft threatened them and no anti-aircraft fire ripped through the slow-moving gliders and transports. The fleet of aircraft continued about its task unmolested. First thoughts were that this landing would attack the rear of the exposed panzer group and this conclusion was reinforced when British tanks attacked Cresserons that evening. Faced with a seemingly hopeless situation, Battle Group *Rauch* withdrew along its route to the relative safety of the division's original assembly area. One company could not make the withdrawal and was forced over to the west where it joined up with the garrison of 230 *Luftwaffe* ground troops inside the still

D-Day Infantry Casualties, 3rd Infantry Division

	Killed	Wounded	Missing
8th Infantry Brigade (assault brigade)			
I S Lancs	18	89	19
2 E Yorks	65	141	3
I Suffolks	7	25	–
185th Infantry Brigade (follow-up brigade)			
2 KSLI	total of 113 killed, wounded and missing		
2 Warwicks	4	35	–
I Norfolks	20	60	–
9th Infantry Brigade (reserve brigade)			
Figures not available for D-Day, but losses in all three battalions were slight.			
Divisional machine-gun battalion			
2 Middlesex	3	26	7

uncaptured radar station at Douvres (a Juno Beach objective), where it remained fighting with the airmen for the next 11 days.

Feuchtinger and Marcks were also startled by this new development and decided to withdraw 21st Panzer Division into defensive positions along the line Hérouville–Lébisey–Épron for the night. The armoured attack against the landings, so necessary in Rommel's view to destroy the invasion, had failed. Every moment that the Allies remained unmolested their strength would increase. Marcks was correct in his assumption that, if the attack did not sweep the British into the sea, then it would likely be impossible ever to do so. The strength of the Allied air forces had been amply demonstrated. With no real *Luftwaffe* force able to counter this supremacy, the skies belonged to the invader.

There was little left of 716th Infantry Division in front of Caen. Some strongpoints manned by 736th Grenadier Regiment still held out, notably in Lion-sur-Mer and Luc-sur-Mer. A few survivors from the three battalions of 736th Grenadier Regiment had made their way towards the divisional command post in the stone quarries of la Folie on the outskirts of Caen, and Lieutenant Schaaf had brought his mobile 10th Battery south to report to 716th Infantry Division's artillery headquarters. He was told that his battery was the only one to make contact with headquarters since morning out of the ten with which the regiment that had started the action. The others had all disappeared under the weight of the Allied assault and air bombardment.

GenLt Richter's division had performed quite well against the

Sword Beach landings and had done all that could have been reasonably expected, considering the calibre of its troops and the widespread dispersal of its positions. Its men had resisted a ferocious and well-organised onslaught by some of the best-trained and equipped Allied troops. The fact that it had crumbled under this massive attack was not surprising, but it had slowed the invasion to a point whereby the capture of Caen on this first day became unrealistic. Rommel could not really have asked for more from a 'static' division. The responsibility for the German failure to defeat the landings lay much higher up the chain of command than GenLt Richter and his men.

CHAPTER 5

THE MOVE ON CAEN

During the late afternoon of 6 June, the German Armed Forces High Command finally released both 12th SS Panzer Division *Hitlerjugend* and the Panzer Lehr Division to Rommel's Army Group B for use by Seventh Army. Initially they were to be attached to Marcks' LXXXIV Corps for immediate deployment, but later in the day this order was changed when I SS Panzer Corps was activated under the command of *SS-Obergruppenführer* (General) Josef 'Sepp' Dietrich. The 12th SS and Panzer Lehr Divisions, together with 21st Panzer and 716th Infantry Divisions were now to be grouped in I SS Panzer Corps and given responsibility for the sector to the right of LXXXIV Corps, that is the area around Caen. The new corps boundary was to run along the line of 716th Infantry Division's original divisional boundary.

These moves would eventually bring one infantry and three panzer divisions into the line against British 3rd and Canadian 3rd Infantry Divisions and the follow-up 51st (Highland) and 7th Armoured Divisions, when they had completed their landings on 8 June. The Germans were now, at last, massing their available armour to drive the British and Canadians back into the sea. Before an attack could be launched, however, the panzer divisions would have to be brought into the line over roads dominated by Allied air power.

HISTORY

When night fell on 6 June, the Sword Beach lodgement stretched in a semi-circle from Lion-sur-Mer in the west, to the west of Hermanville, Point 61, and Biéville, to the edge of the Orne canal at Blainville. 185th Infantry Brigade held the most southerly positions, 9th Infantry Brigade was in the sector behind it and 8th Infantry Brigade had congregated around Hermanville. To the left, 6th Airborne Division held an area east of the Orne centred on Ranville. Canadian 3rd Infantry Division from Juno Beach had advanced roughly the same distance inland as its British counterpart and its forward positions were in the vicinity of Villons-les-Buissons, about 5 km west of Biéville. Between the two Allied divisions was the open strip of countryside between Caen and the sea, which 21st Panzer Division had exploited. It was still an area devoid of any Allied troops, for the landings on Sword and Juno had not yet been joined. Some German troops were still in the gap in the early evening, but they had not made their presence felt. On 7 June the Germans planned to try to get through to the sea again with stronger forces.

The advanced units of 12th SS Panzer Division had arrived to the south of Caen during the night after a march fraught with danger from the air. *SS-Standartenführer* (Colonel) Kurt Meyer had pushed on ahead of his 25th SS Panzergrenadier Regiment and reported to GenLt Richter's HQ in his underground bunker

Generalmajor Edgar Feuchtinger, commander of 21st Panzer Division. (Bundesarchiv 146/87/1201/19a)

at la Folie. There he met with the commander of 716th Infantry Division and with GenMaj Feuchtinger. The two tired generals briefed the young colonel on the situation and the setbacks suffered since the landings. Whilst at Richter's HQ, Meyer received a call from his divisional commander, *SS-Brigadeführer* (Major-General) Fritz Witt, telling him that I SS Panzer Corps had ordered an attack to be launched at 1600 hours the next day, 7 June. The 12th SS and 21st Panzer Divisions were to move against the Allied landings. The two armoured units were to advance on either side of the Caen–Luc-sur-Mer railway line and push the invaders into the sea. Witt realised that his full division would not be available for this attack as most of it was still on the move into the area. Some units were not expected until nightfall on 7 June but Meyer was told that the attack would have to go ahead regardless. He was to form as much of the division as had arrived into a battle group under his command and attack as ordered.

The night of 6 June was also busy for the British. Gains had to be consolidated and preparations made to receive the inevitable German counter-attack. Lt-Gen Dempsey knew that the lodgement of his Second Army would have to expand as quickly as possible to accommodate the vast amounts of men and matériel that were being ferried across the Channel from Britain. The landings over Gold and Juno Beaches were going well. British 50th Infantry Division had advanced from Gold to the outskirts of Bayeux and the Canadians had moved 10 km inland from Juno to close on the vitally important airfield at Carpiquet to the west of Caen. 7th Armoured and 51st (Highland) Divisions would start coming ashore on 7 June. General Montgomery was still pushing for Caen to be taken, urging Dempsey to keep up the momentum with Canadian 3rd Infantry Division and British 3rd Infantry Division. Both were to continue the attack at first light.

Staff from GenLt Richter's headquarters outside his command post in the quarry at la Folie to the north-west of Caen, now the site of the Mémorial de Caen. *(Private Collection/Archives du Mémorial de Caen)*

British 3rd Infantry Division resumed its advance on Caen on 7 June with 185th Infantry Brigade. Leading the brigade's attack was 2 Warwicks which had been ordered to take Lébisey Wood prior to the rest of the brigade's attack on Lébisey village. The three battalions would then push on towards Caen. 2 Warwicks had spent the night by the Orne canal just to the north of Blainville, with one company back in Bénouville. As a preliminary to its attack, 2 Warwicks moved forward and cleared Blainville and then headed south to its start line along the small rivulet called the Dan. The attack was planned to begin at 0845 hours, but when 2 Warwicks tried to get its carriers and anti-tank guns down to the stream they became bogged down in the swampy ground. The battalion commander, Lt-Col H.O.S. Herdon, decided to postpone the attack for an hour and instructed the artillery to delay the start of their supporting barrage. Unfortunately, the two attacking companies did not get this information and set out as ordered at 0845 hours. They advanced through the cornfields and up the long slopes leading to Lébisey Wood without any fire from the preliminary bombardment or their close-support weapons.

Confronted with this misunderstanding, Lt-Col Herdon decided to press on with the battalion attack without the concerted fire-plan. He sent his carriers and anti-tank guns around through Biéville and ordered them to come up to the wood along the road from the north when summoned. He then moved his third company and his headquarters forward to the start line and struck out with them to join the other companies in the wood a kilometre away. All went well until the leading troops were just 200 metres from the edge of the trees. The whole ridge had been taken over by a battalion of Feuchtinger's 125th Panzergrenadier Regiment and these troops were now safely established in trench positions watching the men of 2 Warwicks as they moved directly towards them. The Germans opened up with small arms fire and scythed gaps through the Warwicks' ranks. There was no cover on the hillside so the infantry had to rush at the enemy amongst the trees to have a chance of survival.

The two leading companies got into Lébisey Wood and came to grips with the panzergrenadiers at close quarters. The concentrated German fire made it difficult to make much progress through the trees and most of the men of 2 Warwicks were pinned down near the fringes of the wood. The third

Panzer IV from 6th Company, 12th SS Panzer Regiment, part of 12th SS Panzer Division *Hitlerjugend*. The crew have painted their girlfriends' names on the tank; the commander's girl was evidently called Wilma and the driver's sweetheart was Paula. *(Bundesarchiv 101/297/1722/28)*

company followed the first two into the mêlée and all spent the next few hours just trying to stay alive under a welter of mortar and machine-gun fire. On the corn-covered slopes outside the wood, Lt-Col Herdon's carrier was hit by a burst of machine-gun fire and he was killed. The fight dragged on all morning and into the afternoon until 1500 hours, when the battalion's fourth company came up and joined in the battle. It succeeded in getting into the north-east corner of the wood and cleared a good many of the panzergrenadiers from their positions, but the new impetus did little to make 2 Warwicks' hold on the area any more secure.

By this time it was clear to Brigadier Smith that 2 Warwicks could not capture Lébisey Wood unaided. Most of the day had been wasted waiting for them to do so. He now committed 1 Norfolks to the battle at 1600 hours, with orders to capture the village of Lébisey and to relieve 2 Warwicks. 1 Norfolks advanced up the slopes to the wood in good order, with the battalion mortars and anti-tank guns firing in support. Progress was slow in the face of heavy return fire; machine-guns and mortar shells tore into the ranks. The leading two companies reached the edge of the wood, but could not get further inside

A 4.2-inch mortar of 2 Middlesex, 3rd Infantry Division's machine-gun and mortar battalion, firing in support of an attack from a position near Biéville. *(IWM B5577)*

than the outer fringe. They were forced to endure the same frustrations that 2 Warwicks had suffered since morning. The woods were held in force by well-entrenched panzergrenadiers and their fire was too severe and accurate to counter effectively. Two battalions were now in the wood and neither could make any impression. By early evening, Smith had lost all hope of a successful outcome from the move and ordered a complete withdrawal of his battalions from their exposed positions back to the brigade's lines in Biéville. The fighting had cost 2 Warwicks 154 casualties and 1 Norfolks almost 50. 185th Infantry Brigade had made a second attempt to reach Caen and had failed again.

Maj-Gen Rennie had also committed 9th Infantry Brigade to the drive for Caen. Its axis was along the route Périers-sur-le-Dan–Mathieu–le Mesnil–Cambes-en-Plaine. 2 RUR led the advance, moving over the ridge from west of Point 61 and sweeping down into Périers. The Ulstermen found the village clear and 1 KOSB moved through them to take up the lead. Mathieu was also passed without opposition and at around 1230 hours 1 KOSB pushed on down the road towards Caen. Just out of the village the battalion moved to the right and entered the hamlet of le Mesnil and concentrated in its small wood. The village of Cambes lay just 1 km away along a dusty track. Between le Mesnil and Cambes was the railway line which ran from Caen to Luc-sur-Mer. On 7 June this formed the boundary between 12th SS and 21st Panzer Divisions.

The arrival of 1 KOSB in le Mesnil alarmed 21st Panzer Division most of all, for the British battalion now sat squarely across the route down which the division was preparing to advance that afternoon. The move of 9th Infantry Brigade into the area meant that Feuchtinger had to deal with two attacks – 1 Norfolks and 2 Warwicks were still causing him trouble at Lébisey – at the very moment that he was organising his own. Artillery and mortar fire now descended on the men of 1 KOSB as they dug slit trenches in the wood at le Mesnil. During the early afternoon, at around 1400 hours after a period of unremitting shell fire, 2 RUR came up to join 1 KOSB in the tiny village. The Ulstermen were now to take up the lead once again and push forward and capture Cambes. Unbeknown to their commanding officer, Lt-Col I.C. Harris, the young panzer-grenadiers of 12th SS Panzer Division were also closing on Cambes from the opposite side of the village.

Maj-Gen Tom Rennie, commander British 3rd Infantry Division. Rennie was wounded on 13 June, but returned to service in command of 51st (Highland) Division. He was killed just before the Rhine crossings in March 1945. *(IWM H38083)*

Colonel Meyer had set up his advance headquarters in Ardennes Abbey, just 5 km west of central Caen. Here he had gathered together a battle group formed from those elements of 12th SS Panzer Division that had completed their march to the invasion area. It consisted of all three battalions of his 25th SS Panzergrenadier Regiment; most of 2nd Battalion, 12th SS Panzer Regiment – though only 50 of the battalion's 90 Panzer IVs had arrived in time; and 3rd Battalion, 12th SS Artillery Regiment.

Meyer was supposed to launch his attack in concert with

A battery of self-propelled guns from one of the field regiments of British 3rd Infantry Division, ready to fire in support of the infantry. *(IWM B5032)*

that of 21st Panzer Division at 1600 hours, but events forced his hand two hours earlier when tanks from Canadian 3rd Infantry Division approached his assembly areas around Ardennes Abbey and Carpiquet. The Canadians had continued their advance inland earlier that morning and had made remarkably good progress. Moving south from Villons-les-Buissons, the North Nova Scotia Highlanders easily took Buron from stragglers of 716th Infantry Division around midday and pressed on to Authie. To their left, tanks of the Sherbrooke Fusiliers (27th Canadian Armoured Regiment) moved around to the east of Authie and in so doing were heading across the face of Battle Group *Meyer*'s headquarters in Ardennes Abbey. Meyer watched the battlefield from one of the two towers of the medieval abbey. The tanks continued south and reached the outskirts of Franqueville at 1400 hours. Here they almost ran into the first of Meyer's panzers. The strung-out line of Canadian tanks and infantry were too tempting a target and Meyer gave the order to open fire. The results were devastating for the Canadians. After a furious fire-fight lasting many hours, and with great losses suffered on both sides, the Canadians were forced to retreat through Authie and Buron, back almost to their start line.

Meyer had been drawn into the attack two hours too soon, prompted to act by the Canadian advance. Feuchtinger had also been embroiled over on the right flank by British 3rd Infantry Division. Neither could now attack as planned. Meyer, however, still had his 1st and 2nd Battalions, 25th SS Panzergrenadiers, and at 1500 hours he sent them north against St-Contest, Galmanche and Cambes. 2nd Battalion attacked first and took St-Contest with few problems, but did lose its battalion commander, then moved on to Galmanche. 1st Battalion began its attack on the southern edge of Cambes at 1615 hours, supported by five Panzer IVs of 8th Company, 12th SS Panzer Regiment. The attackers got into the village centre and then the wood to the north, which was surrounded by a high stone wall.

Signallers from 3rd Infantry Division make contact with the division's field artillery to request support fire against a German position. *(IWM B5065)*

No sooner had the SS troops got themselves established than a British artillery barrage descended, heralding the start of 2 RUR's attack. 2 RUR sent one company down the track from le Mesnil behind this barrage at 1700 hours, supported by a squadron of tanks from the East Riding Yeomanry. It did so in the face of terrific artillery and mortar fire. The Ulstermen got into the village, but could not hold it and were evicted with great loss. 2 RUR tried again on 9 June, with the whole battalion advancing in open order across the fields from Anisy. This time it was they who evicted the SS men and established a hold on the wood inside its massive stone wall. Here the battalion remained, relieved in turn by other units, until the start of Operation 'Charnwood' on 8 July, when an all-out push for Caen began.

Three days into the invasion, the advance from Sword Beach had come to a halt. Caen had not been taken on D-Day as planned and 3rd Infantry Division's troops had not got any closer to the city than their precarious hold on the line around Cambes and Biéville on 9 June. In spite of this initial setback, the landings over Sword Beach must be seen as a spectacular success. The 3rd Infantry Division had broken through Hitler's vaunted Atlantic Wall and carved out a lodgement large enough for follow-up divisions to deploy through, with comparatively light casualties.

The campaign in Normandy that followed was a much bloodier affair. The presence of 21st Panzer Division, and its reinforcement by the 12th SS Panzer and Panzer Lehr Divisions, stopped Montgomery's advance stone dead. The build-up of German forces over the next few weeks almost matched that of the Allies. Further progress could only be made by employing overwhelming force and by enduring a grinding war of attrition. Caen would not be taken until mid-July. By then the city had been reduced to a pile of smoking rubble. It would be another six weeks before the whole German line broke and the Allies fought their way out of Normandy.

A Marauder medium bomber from the US 9th Air Force flies over Sword Beach. The road inland to Colleville is seen on the left of the picture, with strongpoint Cod in the centre and Lion-sur-Mer to the right. *(US National Archives)*

PART THREE

BATTLEFIELD
TOURS

GENERAL TOURING INFORMATION

Normandy is a thriving holiday area, with some beautiful countryside, excellent beaches and very attractive architecture (particularly in the case of religious buildings). It was also, of course, the scene of heavy fighting in 1944, and this has had a considerable impact on the tourist industry. To make the most of your trip, especially if you intend visiting non-battlefield sites, we strongly recommend you purchase one of the general Normandy guidebooks that are commonly available. These include: *Michelin Green Guide: Normandy*; *Thomas Cook Travellers: Normandy*; *The Rough Guide to Brittany and Normandy*; *Lonely Planet: Normandy*.

TRAVEL REQUIREMENTS

First, make sure you have the proper documentation to enter France as a tourist. Citizens of European Union countries, including Great Britain, should not usually require visas, but will need to carry and show their passports. Others should check with the French Embassy in their own country before travelling. British citizens should also fill in and take Form E111 (available from main post offices), which deals with entitlement to medical treatment, and all should consider taking out comprehensive travel insurance. France is part of the Eurozone, and you should also check exchange rates before travelling.

GETTING THERE

The most direct routes from the UK to Lower Normandy are by ferry from Portsmouth to Ouistreham (near Caen), and from Portsmouth or Poole to Cherbourg. Depending on which you choose, and whether you travel by day or night, the crossing takes between five and seven hours. Alternatively, you can sail to Le Havre, Boulogne or Calais and drive the rest of the way. (Travel time from Calais to Caen is about four hours; motorway

Above: A Churchill AVRE on display outside Lion-sur-Mer. Three of these tanks were knocked out by an anti-tank gun within a few hundred metres of this monument when trying to attack strongpoint Trout. *(Author)*

Page 97: A disabled Crab flail tank from 79th Armoured Division on the beach near the western end of Queen White sector. Beside the tank steel matting has been laid on the sand to form a firm path towards the beach exit. *(IWM B5192)*

and bridge tolls may be payable depending on the exact route taken.) Another option is to use the Channel Tunnel. Whichever way you choose to travel, early booking is advised, especially during the summer months.

Although you can of course hire motor vehicles in Normandy, the majority of visitors from the UK or other EU countries will probably take their own. If you do so, you will also need to take: a full driving licence; your vehicle registration document; a certificate of motor insurance valid in France (your insurer will advise on this); spare headlight and indicator bulbs; headlight beam adjusters or tape; a warning triangle; and a sticker or number plate identifying which country the vehicle is registered in. Visitors from elsewhere should consult a motoring organisation in their home country for details of the documents and other items they will require.

The Normandy road system is well developed, although there are still a few choke points, especially around the larger towns during rush hour and in the holiday season. As a general guide, in clear conditions it is possible to drive from Cherbourg to Caen in less than two hours.

Centaur IV tank armed with a 95-mm howitzer. These tanks were manned by Royal Marines from the armoured support group and were intended to give covering fire to the infantry from LCT(A)s during the run-in to the beaches. They were then available to provide close support during the subsequent enlargement of the beachhead. *(IWM B5457)*

ACCOMMODATION

Accommodation in Normandy is plentiful and diverse, from cheap campsites to five star hotels in glorious châteaux. However, early booking is advised if you wish to travel between June and August. There is no shortage of places to stay in the Sword Beach area and, as you would expect from a holiday region, there are plenty of good cafés and restaurants nearby. All of the seaside towns have hotels, mostly small to medium in size and rather reminiscent of an earlier age. Nonetheless, they are welcoming, comfortable and often complete with their own excellent restaurants. Most towns in the area have websites where you can find available hotels and compare prices and facilities before you book. For those who wish to stay in modern large hotels that are usually part of a chain or group, there are quite a number located just a few kilometres inland around Caen, just inside the ring road. There are four or five within a kilometre of the Mémorial de Caen alone. These offer a full range of facilities and are clean and comfortable, if a little impersonal. The excellent network of roads nearby makes access to Sword Beach from Caen extremely easy.

If you decide to pay a sudden visit to the area without booking in advance, then all of the local tourist offices (*Les Syndicats d'Initiatives*) have leaflets listing nearby hotels and will help you locate a suitable place to stay. An alternative is to consider renting a *gîte* or apartment and making your stay a little longer, combining a beach holiday with a pilgrimage to the battlefields. Brittany Ferries supply a brochure listing some of those available in the area, as do other ferry and travel companies.

Useful contacts include:

French Travel Centre, 178 Piccadilly, London W1V 0AL;
  tel: 0870 830 2000; web: www.raileurope.co.uk
Calvados Tourisme, Place du Canada, 14000 Caen;
  tel: +33 (0)2 31 86 53 30; web: www.calvados-tourisme.com
Manche Tourisme; web: www.manchetourisme.com
Maison du Tourisme de Cherbourg et du Haut-Cotentin,
  2 Quai Alexandre III, 50100 Cherbourg-Octeville;
  tel: +33 (0)2 33 93 52 02; web: www.ot-cherbourg-cotentin.fr
Gîtes de France, La Maison des Gîtes de France et du Tourisme
  Vert, 59 rue Saint-Lazare, 75 439 Paris Cedex 09;
  tel: +33 (0)1 49 70 75 75; web: www.gites-de-france.fr

BATTLEFIELD TOURING

Each volume in the 'Battle Zone Normandy' series contains from four to six battlefield tours. These are intended to last from a few hours to a full day apiece. Some are best undertaken using motor transport, others should be done on foot, and many involve a mixture of the two. Owing to its excellent infrastructure and relatively gentle topography, Normandy also makes a good location for a cycling holiday; indeed, some of our tours are ideally suited to this method.

In every case the tour author has visited the area concerned recently, so the information presented should be accurate and reasonably up to date. Nevertheless land use, infrastructure and rights of way can change, sometimes at short notice. If you encounter difficulties in following any tour, we would very much like to hear about it, so we can incorporate changes in future editions. Your comments should be sent to the publisher at the address provided at the front of this book.

To derive maximum value and enjoyment from the tours, we suggest you equip yourself with the following items:

- Appropriate maps. European road atlases can be purchased from a wide range of locations outside France. However, for navigation within Normandy, the French Institut Géographique National (IGN <www.ign.fr>) produces maps at a variety of scales. The 1:100,000 series ('Top 100') is particularly useful when driving over larger distances; sheet 06 (Caen – Cherbourg) covers most of the invasion area. For pinpointing locations precisely, the current IGN 1:25,000 Série Bleue is best (we use extracts from this series for the tour maps in this book). These can be purchased in many places across Normandy. They can also be ordered in the UK from some high street bookshops, or from specialist map dealers such as the Hereford Map Centre, 24–25 Church Street, Hereford HR1 2LR; tel: 01432 266322; web: <www.themapcentre.com>. Allow at least a fortnight's notice, although some maps may be in stock.
- Lightweight waterproof clothing and robust footwear are essential, especially for touring in the countryside.
- Take a compass, provided you know how to use one!
- A camera and spare films/memory cards.
- A notebook and writing materials to record what you have photographed.
- A French dictionary and/or phrasebook. (English is widely spoken in the coastal area, but is much less common inland.)
- Food and drink. Although you are never very far in Normandy from a shop, restaurant or *tabac*, many of the tours do not pass directly by such facilities. It is therefore sensible to take some light refreshment with you.
- Binoculars. Most officers and some other ranks carried binoculars in 1944. Taking a pair adds a surprising amount of verisimilitude to the touring experience.

SOME DO'S AND DON'TS

Battlefield touring can be an extremely interesting and even emotional experience, especially if you have read something about the battles beforehand. In addition, it is fair to say that residents of Normandy are used to visitors, among them battlefield tourists, and generally will do their best to help if you encounter problems. However, many of the tours in the 'Battle Zone Normandy' series are off the beaten track, and you can expect some puzzled looks from the locals, especially inland. In all cases we have tried to ensure that tours are on public land, or viewable from public rights of way. In the unlikely event that you are asked to leave a site, do so immediately and by the most direct route.

Infantry from one of the beach groups by their shelters at the top of Queen White Beach the day after the landings. The prominent building in the background was a peacetime hotel which has now been demolished, but it allows us to put the location of this picture as being around 200 metres to the east of the present-day Place du Cuirassé Courbet. *(IWM B5181)*

In addition: **Never remove 'souvenirs' from the battlefields.** Even today it is not unknown for farmers to turn up relics of the 1944 fighting. Taking these without permission may not only be illegal, but can be extremely dangerous. It also ruins the site for genuine battlefield archaeologists. Anyone returning from France should also remember customs regulations on the import of weapons and ammunition of any kind.

BATTLEFIELD TOURS

Be especially careful when investigating fortifications. Some of the more frequently-visited sites are well preserved, and several of them have excellent museums. However, both along the coast and inland, there are numerous positions that have been left to decay, and which carry risks for the unwary. In particular, remember that many of these places were the scenes of heavy fighting or subsequent demolitions, which may have caused severe (and sometimes invisible) structural damage. Coastal erosion has also undermined the foundations of a number of shoreline defences. Under no circumstances should underground bunkers, chambers and tunnels be entered, and care should always be taken when examining above-ground structures. If in any doubt, stay away.

Beware of hunting (shooting) areas (signposted *Chasse Gardée*). Do not enter these, even if they offer a short cut to your destination. Similarly, Normandy contains a number of restricted areas (military facilities and wildlife reserves), which should be avoided. Watch out, too, for temporary footpath closures, especially along sections of coastal cliffs.

If using a motor vehicle, keep your eyes on the road. There are many places to park, even on minor routes, and it is always better to turn round and retrace your path than to cause an accident. In rural areas avoid blocking entrances and driving along farm tracks; again, it is better to walk a few hundred metres than to cause damage and offence.

All of the tours in this book, bar the first, are designed for car or cycle. They are all relatively short, with the longest only around 27 km (16 miles). The starting point for all tours is Ouistreham at the mouth of the River Orne and all finish no more than a few kilometres away. Sword Beach is actually situated virtually alongside the ferry terminal used by Brittany Ferries' Caen–Portsmouth service, with the site of the gun battery at Ouistreham/Riva Bella just a few hundred metres away. To the west of the town are the seaside villages and towns of Lion-sur-Mer, Luc-sur-Mer, Langrune and St-Aubin-sur-Mer, all of which are thriving holiday resorts in the summer. Out of season they are perfect places to walk, explore and enjoy exercise, fresh air and good food.

The beaches here are excellent for families as they are wide, flat and sandy. None are over-commercialised, and the resorts rely more on the natural attractions of sun, sea and sand than on fun fairs and candy floss. In the evenings, the casinos at Riva

Bella, Luc-sur-Mer and St-Aubin-sur-Mer offer a different type of entertainment. All along the coast here, and especially along Queen sector of Sword Beach, it is still possible to drive your car right up to the edge of the sands, park without payment, and enjoy a day at the seaside. Further along the coast to the west, the gentle pace of these summer resorts continues along the British and Canadian D-Day landing beaches of Juno and Gold. Further

Le Grand Bunker Musée le Mur de l'Atlantique – the Atlantic Wall Museum – is housed in a former coastal observation bunker at Ouistreham. It is one of the best museums on the whole Overlord coastline. The building is contemporary to the invasion, contains a fascinating collection of German artefacts, and is preserved and equipped just as it was in 1944. *(Author)*

west still, for those with a little more time, the American landings at Omaha and Utah are within an hour's drive.

For those who wish to experience more of Normandy than the 1944 battlefields, the area is also rich in more distant relics of the past, together with many modern attractions. As always, the local tourist office should be your first port of call, to pick up leaflets describing suitable places to visit. Caen and Bayeux are excellent venues in which to spend a day; both are full of cultural sites, fascinating buildings, interesting streets and wonderful restaurants. There are thriving markets at Caen, Ouistreham/Riva Bella and Courseulles, selling a full range of fresh Norman produce and other items.

Memorial to Captain Kieffer and his French commandos on the corner of the D514 and Avenue du 4ème Commando in Colleville-Montgomery Plage. The large house in the background is the old Château de Colleville Plage. *(Author)*

For the military-minded, in addition to those museums and war cemeteries mentioned in the tours, there are a number of nearby attractions to add to your itinerary. These include: the *Mémorial de Caen* (the Nobel Gallery of this museum is actually situated in GenLt Richter's underground divisional headquarters bunker, located on this site in 1944); the *Merville Battery Museum*; the *Radar Museum* at Douvres-la-Délivrande; the

D-Day Museum at Arromanches; the *Battle of Normandy Museum* at Bayeux; and the new *Juno Beach Centre* at Courseulles. Further afield, there are many more excellent museums relating to the fighting in Normandy. Again, go to the local tourist office and pick up the booklet 'The D-Day Landings and the Battle of Normandy', which lists 35 museums and sites worthy of a visit.

As far as the Sword Beach tours are concerned you may well find that the very best time to undertake these is in the early afternoon or early evening (seasons permitting) when the locals are at home preoccupied with their food. Certainly the time to avoid Caen is the rush hour, when every side road and country lane is used as a short-cut by anxious and manic commuters.

You will find a good local map useful, such as sheet 1612 OT of the Institut Géographique National Série Bleue 1:25,000 series. This map covers all the places included in these tours.

The statue of Field Marshal Montgomery beside the D514 road at Colleville-Montgomery Plage, the starting point for all of the Sword Beach tours. *(Author)*

STARTING POINT FOR ALL TOURS: is the statue of Field Marshal Montgomery to the rear of Sword Beach alongside the D514 road. The statue stands close by the traffic lights just off the junction of the main road, the D514, and the road which leads inland to Colleville-Montgomery, the D60a. This area is now called Colleville-Montgomery Plage. The D514 runs along the rear of the beach from Ouistreham to Lion-sur-Mer. You can park in the side road beside the statue.

To reach the D514 from Caen leave the city's northern ring road, the N413, at its junction with the D515. Follow this road to Bénouville, where it becomes the D514, and continue north to Ouistreham and then Colleville-Montgomery Plage.

TOUR A

QUEEN SECTOR OF SWORD BEACH

OBJECTIVE: This tour takes us along the length of Queen sector of Sword Beach, the landing site of British 3rd Infantry Division on D-Day. It visits the parts of the beach where the initial assault waves of 2 E Yorks and 1 S Lancs came ashore and the site of the landings made by the commandos of Lord Lovat's 1st Special Service Brigade. The tour also covers the exit routes made from the beach, German fortifications and the locations of buildings and sites contemporary with the landings.

Looking across from Queen Red sector of Sword Beach towards Queen White sector, the dunes still remain as they were when 8th Infantry Brigade stormed ashore. In the distance the bay sweeps round to Lion-sur-Mer. Strongpoint Trout was located on the extreme right of the picture. *(Author)*

DURATION/SUITABILITY: The distance covered is about 2 km and the tour will probably take about 2 hours. For the cyclist or walker this is an excellent tour along a flat traffic-free beach road. For the disabled it is also a good tour with access close to all major sites followed by a minimal amount of walking.

Unfortunately, it is not possible to drive the length of Sword Beach along the seafront road. It is necessary, therefore, to use

① Queen Green sector
② Queen White sector
③ Queen Red sector
④ Roger Green sector
⑤ 1 S Lancs' landing area
⑥ 41 RM Commando's landing site
⑦ 2 E Yorks' landing area
⑧ 1st Special Service Brigade's landing area

ⓐ Statue of FM Montgomery
ⓑ Avenue du 4ème Commando
ⓒ Eighteenth century redoubt
ⓓ Pre-war holiday camp
ⓔ Rue de Pont l'Évêque
ⓕ Rue de Rouen
ⓖ Place de la 3ème D.I.B.
ⓗ Avenue Felix Faure
ⓘ Place de Cuirassé Courbet
ⓙ Centaur tank

Base map: IGN 1612OT

the main Ouistreham–Lion-sur-Mer road, located slightly inland, to move lengthwise along the beach, then pass down small side roads to reach the appropriate points along the shore.

DIRECTIONS ON FOOT: With the Montgomery statue behind you cross the main road towards the beach and take the right hand road opposite, called Avenue du 4ème Commando.

DIRECTIONS BY CAR: From the statue proceed a few metres northwards towards the sea to the traffic lights on the main road, the D514, that runs behind the statue. Turn right towards Ouistreham and then turn immediately left into Avenue du 4ème Commando and park where safe.

THE SITE: Immediately on the right is an early post-war monument to the landings, marking the site of the temporary first graves of men killed on 6 June 1944. On the opposite side of the road is a memorial to Captain Kieffer and his French commandos whose route to their D-Day objective passed this point and continued eastwards along the D514 towards Ouistreham.

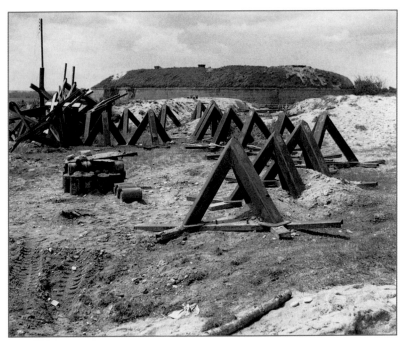

Beach obstacles dumped at the top of the beach. In the background is the 18th century redoubt, used as part of the beach defences. *(IWM B6376)*

The 18th century redoubt at Colleville Plage. The Germans fortified this venerable coast defence position and mounted weapons on its roof. *(Author)*

DIRECTIONS ON FOOT/BY CAR: Continue along the Avenue du 4ème Commando towards the sea. Take the next left into Rue de la Redoute and continue along it for a short distance.

THE SITE: On the left, behind the houses, is a grass-topped late-18th century coastal fortification, which guarded the port of Ouistreham. The Germans fortified it and placed machine guns on its roof. This small fort appears in some of the contemporary photographs of the landings (*see picture opposite*).

DIRECTIONS ON FOOT: Turn to the right, go down the steps and continue along the Rue de Vauban for 100 metres, to the sea. This road is named after the architect of so many magnificent European fortifications. You have now arrived at the road running along the top of the beach.

DIRECTIONS BY CAR: Continue to the end of the Rue de la Redoute. Turn right, then first right, then first left. Carry on the short distance to the sea, turn left and park by the memorial.

THE SITE: You are now at the eastern edge of Queen Red Beach, with Roger White Beach to the right. To the east the shore sweeps round to Riva Bella and the ferry port at Ouistreham. The

BATTLEFIELD TOURS

strongpoint at Riva Bella attacked by the French commandos is about 1.5 km along the beach and the gun battery at Ouistreham stormed by 4 Commando another 500 metres further on.

In front is a monument to Captain Kieffer and the commandos of Lord Lovat's 1st Special Service Brigade. The memorial plaque states that Kieffer's men landed as an advance guard, followed by 4, 3, 6 and 45 RM Commandos. The monument explains that before the commandos were assembled, 4 officers and 14 other ranks were killed and 30 men were wounded on the beach, including Captain Kieffer. The actual landing place of the first waves of commandos is a little further to the west.

Opposite this monument is a large gun emplacement, which formed part of strongpoint WN-18. On D-Day this housed a 75-mm gun, which was the main weapon in the resistance post. It was positioned to fire along Sword Beach and was protected from bombardment by warships by a concrete shield on the seaward side. This fortified area was much smaller than that of WN-20 (Cod) further along the beach, and comprised the 75-mm gun, a 50-mm gun, several machine-gun posts, minefields and belts of wire, all sited to protect the exit of the beach that led towards Colleville. It was this type of defensive structure that required the Allies to land armour as close as possible to the assaulting infantry, to give them some protection and support while attacking its fortifications.

The main casemate of WN-18. This concrete emplacement housed a 75-mm gun sited to fire in enfilade along the length of Sword Beach. The reinforced flanking wall on its seaward side made the position impervious to gunfire from warships. It was eventually knocked out by tank fire at close range. *(IWM B6381)*

The 75-mm casemate of German strongpoint WN-18 as it is today. The rear of the emplacement is now built into a house. *(Author)*

Christian Hubbe of 716th Infantry Division was in one of the German bunkers on Sword Beach on D-Day.

'More tanks were shooting at us and all sorts of debris was flying about. Then there was a terrible crash and our bunker filled with smoke. I fell down and saw bodies and I thought it was the end. Then the sergeant came in and helped me up and together we started firing again. We used an undamaged machine gun, but after a short time we heard a lot of noise behind us and realised that the enemy tanks and infantry were in our rear. Suddenly there was a lot more noise and the bunker collapsed. A tank had come up and fired a heavy charge that really destroyed everything. It was dark and filled with choking smoke and I staggered to get out. I could not see my sergeant and found out later that he had been killed.'

Source: Edmund Blandford, *Two Sides of the Beach*, p. 28.

DIRECTIONS ON FOOT: Turn to the left and proceed westwards along the beach road. Next on the left is the Avenue de Bruxelles leading back to Monty's statue. There is a local tourist office here with toilets alongside. Opposite the beach here is a large car park.

DIRECTIONS BY CAR: Continue westwards along the seafront road for 100 metres and park opposite the car park.

THE SITE: You are standing on the location of a pre-war holiday park. Lord Lovat's 1st Special Service Brigade landed here and advanced off the beach and through the park before moving inland to their assembly areas. By 6 June the Germans had mined the ground and protected it with wire and pill-boxes. Lovat's commandos had to fight their way onto the lateral road inland against the Germans here and at WN-18 just to the east. This is where most of Lovat's casualties were suffered.

DIRECTIONS ON FOOT: Continue westwards along the beach road. You are now well into Red Beach sector of Queen Beach and alongside the length of the shoreline assaulted by 2 E Yorks on D-Day. Continue along the road for 200 metres until you reach Rue de Pont l'Évêque.

DIRECTIONS BY CAR: Carry on along the beach road for 200 metres until compelled to turn left by traffic signs, then turn immediately right and go along 50 metres to Rue de Pont l'Évêque. Turn right, head towards the beach and stop where convenient.

THE SITE: You are now at the eastern edge of strongpoint WN-20 (Cod). Further westwards the coastal road swings slightly inland leaving a broader area of grassy bank at the top of the beach, about 20 metres wide. This area between the beach road and the sea was part of the strongpoint and contained an anti-tank gun emplacement, a large concrete casemate containing an 88-mm gun, and several Tobruk machine-gun posts, all linked together with wire entanglements and trenches. Inland from this beach road, running southwards from here to the main Ouistreham–Lion road (D514), was the central part of Cod, containing other concrete emplacements and personnel bunkers with more barbed wire, machine guns and minefields. It was a formidable complex garrisoned by men from 10th Company, 3rd Battalion of Colonel Krug's 736th Grenadier Regiment. The western edge of Cod just past the Rue de Rouen was close to the dividing line between Red and White Beaches.

This strongly fortified position was directly opposite the landing place of the two assault companies of 2 E Yorks.

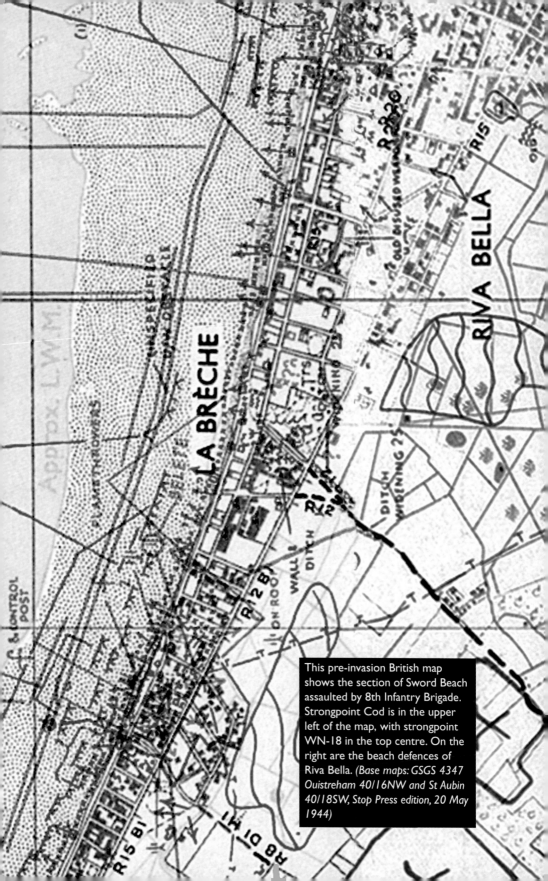

RIVA BELLA

LA BRÈCHE

Appox. L.W.M.

R 28.26

RIS

RIS

FLAME THROWERS

(INSPECFIELD ON DEFILADE)

SELETE

R 12

R 12 B)

(ON ROOF)

WALL & DITCH

DITCH WIDENING 25

DITCH WIDENING 25

C & CONTROL POST

RIS BI

RIS BI

R8 DI MI

This pre-invasion British map shows the section of Sword Beach assaulted by 8th Infantry Brigade. Strongpoint Cod is in the upper left of the map, with strongpoint WN-18 in the top centre. On the right are the beach defences of Riva Bella. *(Base maps: GSGS 4347 Ouistreham 40/16NW and St Aubin 40/18SW, Stop Press edition, 20 May 1944)*

The 88-mm gun casemate at the western edge of strongpoint Cod. The picture was taken by a French civilian from a derelict landing craft some time after the landings. *(Private Collection/Archives du Mémorial de Caen)*

The battalion landed here at 0725 hours on D-Day, midway between high and low tide, into a welter of fire. The infantry left their craft in shallow water and had around 150 metres of sand to cross before they found any shelter. Even then, the only protection from enemy fire was beneath the low sand dunes in front of where you are standing, right under the guns of the German strongpoint. The DD tanks that landed with the infantry, and the tank landing craft that made it to the beach along the areas to the west and the east, all suffered the effects of this close-quarters fire. Gradually, some tanks were able to evade the worst of the shell-fire and came forward to support the infantry in attacking Cod. Even so, it was several hours before all elements of the strongpoint's garrison were eliminated.

Lieutenant K.P. Baxter, 2 Middlesex, recalls his experiences of landing on D-Day.

'The protective steel doors in the bows were opened and everyone waited tensed for the soft lurching bump. "Ramp down!" – and out into knee-deep water. I had not gone far when I was tripped by some underwater wire, and, with no hope of retaining balance in the heavy Assault Jacket that had been issued to us, went flat on my face. Then suddenly the machine gun opened up on us again. The fire came from dead ahead and we could now make out the shape of a heavy embrasure in the low silhouette of some concrete fortifications at the top of the beach. We then realised that, by the narrowest of margins, we had landed immediately in front of strongpoint Cod.'

Source: Warren Tute, John Costello and Terry Hughes, *D-Day,* p. 211.

DIRECTIONS ON FOOT: Turn left and walk down the Rue de Pont l'Évêque until house number 6 on the left just before the main D514 road. On the right hand side of the garden by the house is the only remaining piece of strongpoint Cod, a Tobruk emplacement now used as a garden shed by the owner of the house. Walk back to the promenade and continue westwards to the junction with Rue de Rouen on the left.

DIRECTIONS BY CAR: Return back down the road and join the main Ouistreham-Lion-sur-Mer road. Turn right and continue along to the traffic lights. Turn right into the car park in Place de la 3ème D.I.B (which translates as 3rd British Infantry Division Square), park and walk the few metres to the seafront road. Turn to the right and walk about 50 metres along the beach road to the next road on the right, the Rue de Rouen.

THE SITE: You are now near the western edge of strongpoint Cod. On the corner of the Rue de Rouen is a villa called les Fous de Bassan; it has a road sign outside marked Boulevard de la Mer. Both this villa and the one adjacent to it existed in 1944 and both figure prominently in the background of photographs of the landings.

Go down onto the beach and walk along until you are opposite the houses and compare with the view from the landing craft shown in the picture on pages 44–45. Depending on the state of the tide, you may be able to stand on the spot from which the picture was taken and get a good impression of the assault stages of the landings. Return to the promenade road and continue westwards.

BATTLEFIELD TOURS

You are now crossing from Red Beach to White Beach, into the area where 1 S Lancs landed. The battalion's assault companies attacking this part of the shore lost several officers almost immediately, including the battalion commander, Lt-Col R.P.H. Burbury. The first two companies moved to the west and began to clear the houses along the seafront, while the two follow-up companies landed a little further to the east in front of the right hand end of Cod. Here they were immediately involved in the battle to take the strongpoint.

The next road is the Place de la 3ème D.I.B. and was one of the main exits from the beach on D-Day. The road from here leads inland to Hermanville-sur-Mer. This was the route taken by 8th Infantry Brigade's follow-up battalion, 1 Suffolks, which landed after the assault waves at around 0830 hours.

DIRECTIONS ON FOOT: Continue along the beach road for around 300 metres to Avenue Felix Faure.

DIRECTIONS BY CAR: Leave the car park at Place de la 3ème D.I.B. and turn right onto the main road. Go along about 300 metres until the road begins to swing slightly inland just before the tank. Take the next right, swing left and then immediately turn right into the Avenue Felix Faure. Go to the end of the road.

THE SITE: Alongside the beach road is a memorial to the men of the Royal and Merchant Navies who took part in the invasion. Once the assault phase of the landings was completed, the build-up phase of the invasion began. This involved great numbers of men and quantities of armour, transport, ammunition and equipment landing over the open beaches. Two artificial harbours, called 'Mulberries', were built along the invasion coast, one by the British at Arromanches on Gold Beach and one by the Americans on Omaha Beach. The other three landing beaches, including this one at Sword, were protected by 'Gooseberry' breakwaters. These gave some protection to the minor craft engaged in landing supplies directly onto the shore. The Gooseberry breakwaters consisted of obsolete warships and merchant craft, which were sunk nose to stern in an arc along the two-fathom line off the beach. The shallow waters left the most part of the ships' superstructures above water and these hulks were able to take the main force of any rough weather.

Gooseberry No. 5 was sunk off Sword Beach in the days immediately following the invasion, opposite the point where you are now standing. It consisted of nine blockships, amongst which were the Free French battleship *Courbet*, the British cruiser *Durban* and the Dutch cruiser *Sumatra*.

Part of the 'Gooseberry' breakwater made up of sunken vessels off Sword Beach. The picture was taken from the old French battleship *Courbet*. *(Archives du Mémorial de Caen)*

DIRECTIONS ON FOOT: Carry on for 200 metres to the Place du Cuirassé Courbet and stop by the lifeguard station.

DIRECTIONS BY CAR: Return back down the Avenue Felix Faure and then turn right. Continue for about 150 metres and park on the road. Walk a little further on until the crossroads and bear to the right onto the boardwalk of the Place du Cuirassé Courbet. Walk across the square to the seafront.

THE SITE: This was one of the main exits from the beach, leading directly to the road to Hermanville. It was from a point near here that both 1 S Lancs and 41 RM Commando exited the beach. Leave the beach here, but before moving inland look ahead along the wide sweep of the bay to the west. The houses along the top of the beach merge with the next seafront town of Lion-sur-Mer. Near the eastern end of Lion-sur-Mer, just before the caravan site, is the location of German strongpoint Trout, the

BATTLEFIELD TOURS

Then: An AVRE from 77th Assault Squadron has stopped on its exit from the beach at la Brèche to allow some carriers from 3rd Infantry Division's machine-gun battalion, 2 Middlesex, to turn left from the lateral road towards Hermanville. *(IWM B5040)*

Now: The building on the junction of Place du Cuirassé Courbet and the old lateral road as they are today. *(Author)*

objective of 41 RM Commando. Further westwards can be seen the sandy cliffs lining the shore between Lion and Luc-sur-Mer.

Leave the beach and return to the boardwalk of Place du Cuirassé Courbet. Immediately behind the lifeguard station is the tourist office, which has a small exhibition relating to Sword Beach. Continue to the square. In the centre is a memorial to the midget submarine that was off the beach late on 5 June 1944, ready to surface in the early hours of 6 June and act as a navigation beacon. Alongside is a memorial to British 3rd Infantry Division. On the seaward side of these monuments is a plinth commemorating the ships sunk in the construction of the Gooseberry harbour, with a special mention of Admiral Wietzel, commander of the old French battleship *Courbet*. At the bottom of this monument is a plaque outlining the timings of the D-Day assault. Along the western side of the square are two other monuments, one dedicated to 1 S Lancs and the other to the regiments of the Royal Artillery which landed with 3rd Infantry Division. Set into the ground is a depiction of the division's unit sign, a red triangle inside a large black triangle.

Cross the square away from the beach and stop at the junction with Rue de Dr Turgis. This road was the old lateral road that ran behind the beach, and also the line of the narrow-gauge railway whose tracks can be seen in many D-Day photos. The buildings round this square are also present in many 1944 pictures. A short distance ahead are the traffic lights at the junction of the road to Hermanville (D60b) and the main road from Ouistreham to Lion-sur-Mer (D514). That section of main road was constructed in the post-war period and bypasses this part of the old lateral road. To the right, where the road forks, is the area where 41 RM Commando set up its first HQ, and where Lt-Col Gray gathered together the two groups who were to advance on the château and strongpoint Trout in Lion-sur-Mer.

DIRECTIONS ON FOOT: Turn left and move along the Rue de Dr Turgis in the direction of Ouistreham. Continue for about 150 metres to the point where it meets Avenue Felix Faure from the left and also the D514 road.

DIRECTIONS BY CAR: Return to your car and turn around to go back down the road towards Ouistreham, then stop by the tank 150 metres along on the right.

THE SITE: Nearby are several seats where you can rest while you view the Centaur tank on display by the side of the main road. The tank is dedicated as a memorial to the men of the Royal Marines' assault squadrons, who supported the landings here and elsewhere along the invasion beaches. This type of tank was obsolete by the time of the invasion, but some examples were present in the leading waves of the landings to act as mobile guns. Manned by Royal Marines, they had two distinct roles. First, during the run-in to the shore, they were to fire in support of the assaulting infantry from the decks of the LCT(A)s. Second, once they had left their craft, they were to help attack individual strongpoints and to support the moves off the beach. The Centaurs had bearing indicators painted around their turrets so that the infantry could relay range and directions of possible targets to the commander inside the tank. They were not expected to be used as general battle tanks and were all withdrawn, as planned, soon after the landings. On Sword Beach, 3rd Infantry Division was supported by the Centaur tanks of 5th Battery, Royal Marine Armoured Support Group. At the time of writing the plaque on this memorial related to a previous exhibit and described this tank as an AVRE, which clearly it is not.

THIS IS THE END OF THE TOUR: To return to the start point, walk back westwards along the beach, tide permitting, to the Avenue de Bruxelles and the Ouistreham–Lion road. If driving simply return by the D514 road.

TOUR B

THE PATHS OF 41 RM AND 4 COMMANDOS

OBJECTIVE: This tour follows the routes of 41 RM Commando from Queen White Beach to Lion-sur-Mer and then that taken by 4 Commando from Queen Red Beach to Ouistreham. It visits the strongpoints they attacked and retraces their moves to their other D-Day objectives.

The site of strongpoint Trout at Lion-sur-Mer seen from the beach. This picture can be compared with the contemporary photograph of the German position on page 42 (the same villa is indicated by the arrow). *(Author)*

DURATION/SUITABILITY: The route covers some 15.5 km and will probably take at least 2 hours to complete, plus museum visits. For the cyclist there is good flat ground, but along fairly busy roads. With slight detours, parts of the tour can be covered on cycle paths along the top of the beach. For the disabled, almost all of the important sites can be seen from close to the car, but the tour includes several short walking sections. Disabled access to the tower museums is impossible, unfortunately.

DIRECTIONS: Start the tour at Montgomery's statue as before. Proceed westwards along the D514 towards Lion-sur-Mer. Sword Beach is on the right behind the houses and the D514 road was the main lateral route behind the beach in 1944.

THE SITE: This road soon filled with tanks and vehicles once exits from the beach were opened and massive traffic jams slowed all movement inland. Running alongside this road in 1944 was a narrow-gauge railway line, which can often be seen in contemporary pictures of the landings. On 7 June, Allied engineers ripped up this line to widen the road.

DIRECTIONS: At the first set of traffic lights on the right is one of the main exits from the beach used on D-Day. By this point the

1 Site of the action by three AVRE tanks
2 Limit of 41 RM Commando's advance
3 41 RM Commando's second HQ
4 Attack by 3rd Battalion, 736th Grenadier Regiment
5 Coast defence observation bunker
6 Site of gun battery
7 Harbour outer fortification
a Statue of FM Montgomery
b Lion-sur-Mer church
c AVRE memorial
d Lion-sur-Mer château
e 9th Inf Bde HQ memorial
f Pre-war holiday camp
g Marketplace
h Avenue Pasteur
i Casino
j Eighteen-century redoubt
k Ouistreham Lighthouse
Base map: IGN 1612OT

Sword Beach

Colleville-
-Montgomery Plage

OUISTREHAM

Lion-sur-Mer

Hermanville-
-sur-Mer

0   0.5

road has passed along what was the landward side of German strongpoint Cod. A short distance further on the road curves inland by the Centaur tank mentioned in Tour A. Continue until the next set of traffic lights to reach another of the main exits from the beach.

THE SITE: Just past this junction was 41 RM Commando's assembly point, and its first headquarters after leaving the beach. It was here that the commando formed into two groups for its attacks on strongpoint Trout and the château in Lion-sur-Mer.

The site of strongpoint Trout on the western side of Sword Beach. The buildings on the left were incorporated into the German position. The view is looking eastwards towards the landing beaches on Queen sector. *(Author)*

DIRECTIONS: Go on into Lion-sur-Mer. The first set of traffic lights is in the centre of the town. There is a pedestrianised road to the church on the left and the main part of the old town lies to the right, between here and the sea. Continue through the next set of lights 50 metres further on and up the long straight road.

THE SITE: This was the route taken by the group of commandos attacking Trout. The strongpoint was located ahead at the top of the rise. Along this road, the commandos came under heavy mortar and machine-gun fire from houses on either side of the street and from the strongpoint. Their advance was stopped a few hundred metres from Trout at a point roughly opposite the present-day small supermarket. Following the commandos' call for armoured support, three AVRE tanks from 2nd Troop, 77th Assault Squadron, came forward, only for all three to be knocked out by a well-concealed anti-tank gun within the strongpoint. Without tank support, the commandos could not get any nearer to their objective, and so their attack halted.

Captain A. Low, 2nd Troop, 77th Assault Squadron, RE, commanded an AVRE.

'Our tanks supported the commandos in the attack. Capt McLennen took the first section of 41 RM Commando up the road and I in my AVRE took the second section 20 metres behind, with Lt Tennent in his tank following up the rear. Heavy fire from riflemen in the houses on either side of the street was quietened down by our Besa fire. The loaded Petard bomb in Capt McLennen's tank was hit by bullets and caught fire. His AVRE stopped and was immediately hit by a shell which struck the driver's visor. Then another shell hit his tank, killing Cpl Shea and wounding his driver. The crew abandoned the tank and Capt McLennen was hit by rifle fire and killed. Then Lt Tennent's tank was struck in the turret and his wireless operator killed. It was our turn next, we were hit in the driver's block and then again [in] the turret gun mantlet. Our gunner was killed and the rest of us baled out and joined the commandos by a wall.'

Source: Anon., *Royal Engineers Battlefield Tour: Normandy to the Seine*, p. 78.

DIRECTIONS: Continue along the road and pull off on to the verge about 200 metres before the roundabout, by the Oasis holiday park on your right.

THE SITE: You are now within the fortified area of the German strongpoint. It stretched from the seafront on the right, through the area of the present campsite and across the road. This part of Trout comprised trenches and wire, with dug-in machine-gun posts and mortars. The anti-tank gun that knocked out the three tanks from 79th Armoured Division was sited near here, facing down the road towards the centre of Lion-sur-Mer. The more

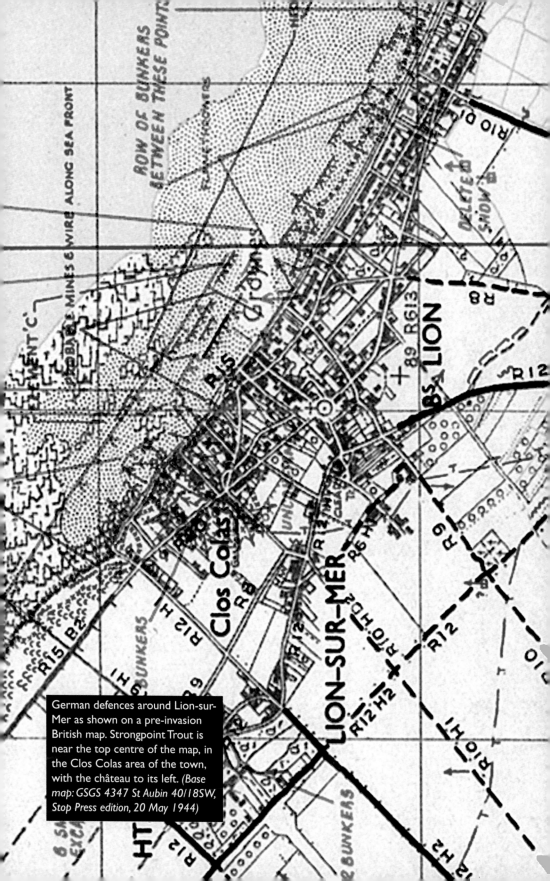

German defences around Lion-sur-Mer as shown on a pre-invasion British map. Strongpoint Trout is near the top centre of the map, in the Clos Colas area of the town, with the château to its left. (Base map: GSGS 4347 St Aubin 40/18SW, Stop Press edition, 20 May 1944)

substantial concrete emplacements of the strongpoint were to the north of here, facing the sea.

DIRECTIONS: Now walk towards the sea through the campsite. To the right, the eastern limit of the fortified area was about 50 metres away. On reaching the seafront promenade, look to the right.

THE SITE: The first house overlooking the sea marks the western end of Trout's heavy emplacements. The low villa with round columns next to it on the corner of Rue de la Hève was built into the fortifications. The photo on page 42 shows this area of the strongpoint from the sea and the arrow points to the villa with the columns (also shown on page 123). If you wish to make a modern comparison, there are steps nearby which lead down to the beach, otherwise return to the car.

Memorial to 41 RM Commando in Hermanville near strongpoint Trout. This position was finally captured on 7 June with the assistance of 2 Lincolns of 9th Infantry Brigade. (Author)

DIRECTIONS: Continue to the roundabout and take the second exit. Park inside the bus and car park. Walk to the Churchill AVRE that stands beside the road to Luc-sur-Mer.

THE SITE: This particular example was presented by General Sir Ian Harris who, as a lieutenant-colonel, commanded 2 RUR on D-Day. The tank is dedicated as a memorial to 41 RM Commando. The AVRE had a large petard mortar as its main weapon, capable of firing a huge charge against concrete emplacements at short range. This example has the unit markings of 79th Armoured Division. It was three AVREs just like this from the division's 77th Assault Squadron that led the attack against strongpoint Trout.

Alongside the tank is a large steel plinth bearing a quotation from President Franklin D. Roosevelt, about the four freedoms: of Speech and Worship, and from Want and Fear. Looking westwards, the next town is Luc-sur-Mer, 1.5 km away. It was on the far side of the town, at Petit Enfer, that 41 and 48 RM Commandos were expected to meet up on D-Day, linking together the landings of Sword and Juno Beaches.

The memorial and preserved Churchill AVRE on the western outskirts of Lion-sur-Mer. *(Author)*

DIRECTIONS: Return to the car and go back to the round-about. Take the southern exit towards Cresserons (D221). Go along the road and across the traffic lights to pass beside a stone wall on the right. Take the next turning on the right. Go on about 200 metres and then pull over to view the château on the right.

THE SITE: You have now reached the château of Lion-sur-Mer, D-Day objective for 41 RM Commando's second group. In 1944 the château was a defended locality with numerous field positions and light weapons. Rommel visited the château and strongpoint Trout on 30 May 1944, just seven days before the invasion, to inspect the local defences and to watch a demonstration of a mobile multi-barrelled mortar. He took lunch at a field kitchen in the grounds.

DIRECTIONS: Carry on to the next junction, turn right and proceed towards the sea. On the left is the open ground over

The Château de Lion-sur-Mer, the D-Day objective of 41 RM Commando. The marines failed to get closer than a few hundred metres to the château before they were counter-attacked during the late morning of 6 June. *(Author)*

which elements of 21st Panzer Division advanced to the coast on the evening of D-Day. Take the next right, skirting the château grounds and proceed back to the traffic lights. Go straight through the junction towards Lion-sur-Mer.

THE SITE: This area was the furthest point reached by the second group of 41 RM Commando during the attack towards the château on D-Day. At the road junction with the lights, the leading commandos of B Troop were halted by fire from the château. A little later, while trying to counter this opposition, the commandos had to switch their attention to deal with a German counter-attack from their left, coming across the open fields from Plumetot. At the same time, German infantry supported by self-propelled guns attacked the rear troop, A Troop, in the flank. The commandos were pulled back from their exposed position, to a new line in the centre of Lion-sur-Mer.

DIRECTIONS: Continue along the road for about 500 metres to the Rue du Stade on the right. This is where A Troop had its positions when the German counter-attack came in. In 1944, all the ground to the right was open country. Most of the buildings on this side of the town are post-war. Continue along the road until just before it bends to the right. On the right is the Rue de Château d'Eau and this marks the position into which 41 RM Commando withdrew on the afternoon of D-Day.

Follow the road round to the right and then take the next left, Rue de Verdun. A short way along on the left is the church. This is where Lt-Col Gray had his commando headquarters. After the counter-attack he moved it further back along the road to Ouistreham. At the junction with the main road, turn right onto the D514 towards Ouistreham. Continue as the road bears round to the left and just past the town sign of Hermanville is a road to the right, called the Chemin du Hamel.

THE SITE: This junction was the position of 9th Infantry Brigade headquarters after it had left the beach at around 1300 hours on 6 June. It was here that brigade headquarters was hit by

Site of the headquarters of 9th Infantry Brigade during the early afternoon of D-Day. Just after it was established, a number of German mortar bombs fell on the command post causing several casualties. The stone memorial on the side of the road commemorates those who were killed or wounded in the attack. *(Author)*

mortar fire and various personnel were killed and wounded. The brigade commander, Brigadier Cunningham, was injured and had to be evacuated. Close by the road junction is a memorial to the men of the headquarters who were killed here. On the opposite side of the main road is the Rue Moulin. Lt-Col Gray moved the headquarters of his commando to an orchard along this road after the German counter-attack on 6 June. The next day his command post was subjected to an air attack, which killed four of his team and wounded nine others, including Gray himself.

This concludes the part of the tour relating to 41 RM Commando.

DIRECTIONS: Continue along the D514 towards Ouistreham, to Monty's statue and the traffic lights at the junction with the D60a road to Colleville. Turn left here and go towards the sea, turning into the car park on the left by the tourist office. The tour now follows the route taken by 4 Commando on D-Day.

THE SITE: This car park is on the location of the former holiday camp fronting Sword Beach. Lovat's commandos landed near here and exited the beach across this ground. First to arrive were Kieffer's French commandos, followed by the remainder of 4 Commando. They all moved inland to the area of Monty's statue then wheeled left and took the main road, Route de Lion, towards Ouistreham. The other commando units of Lord Lovat's 1st Special Service Brigade landed in the second wave, got off the beach near here, crossed the main road near the statue and proceeded southwards over the fields in the direction of Colleville on their way to join up with the airborne troops at Bénouville.

DIRECTIONS: Go back to the traffic lights on the D514 opposite Monty's statue and turn left towards Ouistreham.

THE SITE: Two groups of the French commandos slipped away to the left and moved through the side streets, using the Boulevard Maréchal Joffre as their axis, while the remainder of Kieffer's men and those of 4 Commando pushed on straight down the road. On the right in 1944 was open countryside, much of it flooded by the Germans. 2 E Yorks also advanced along this road before swinging right and moving across to the south to attack strongpoint Sole. About 250 metres along the road on the right is a distinctive stretch of stone wall with a gateway. The picture on page 54 shows troops moving past this point with the supporting DD tanks of 13th/18th Hussars.

DIRECTIONS: Continue eastwards for about 1.5 km through three more sets of traffic lights. Fifty metres before reaching a fourth set, look out for the turning on the left called Avenue Pasteur, which is the road immediately after the open area of the marketplace. Turn left down this road towards the sea.

THE SITE: This is one of the roads that Captain Kieffer's French commandos used to approach the casino strongpoint at Riva

Bella. Other commandos came in from the west along the direction of Boulevard Maréchal Joffre. The main body of 4 Commando continued along the D514 towards Ouistreham and then turned down towards the sea using a number of side roads to approach their main objective, the Riva Bella gun battery further to the east.

The flak tower close by the casino strongpoint position. It now makes an impressive viewing gallery overlooking the beach opposite. *(Author)*

DIRECTIONS: Continue down the tree-lined Avenue Pasteur towards the sea. The bottom of the road is close to the seafront right opposite the new casino. Turn right and go along about 100 metres to the large car park. At the back of the car park, a flight of steps lead up to a stark white multi-legged viewing platform. This is in fact a surviving German flak tower, whose guns provided anti-aircraft protection for the Riva Bella and casino positions.

Now begin a short walking tour of the area, covering about 600 metres. Cross the road from the car park towards the casino, pass to the right of the building and head for the beach.

THE SITE: This casino is on the same site as the pre-war casino and the new building marks the central position of the Riva Bella casino strongpoint. The fortified area stretched on either side of this site and out towards the beach. The casino resistance post was nothing like the building shown in the famous film, *The Longest Day*, for the Germans had demolished it and razed the area before they constructed their fortifications. There were few buildings visible on the surface and most of the fortifications were subterranean, consisting mainly of low weapons bunkers and trench systems.

Concrete 'dragon's teeth' of the anti-tank obstacle to the seaward side of the Riva Bella casino strongpoint. In the upper centre of the picture is the Flame of Sacrifice memorial on top of one of the strongpoint's bunkers. *(Author)*

DIRECTIONS: At the end of the casino, opposite the Hôtel St-George, turn towards the sea between two lines of beach huts. Behind these huts can be seen some concrete dragon's teeth, which formed an anti-tank barrier from the sea and marked the forward edge of the strongpoint. Turn left and walk parallel to the sea, heading towards the Flame of Sacrifice on top of the bunker, which once formed part of the strongpoint's defences. The area to the left, at the back of the hospital, is a section of environmentally-protected dunes that gives a good impression of the natural state of the beach in 1944. Continue along the beach for 200 metres to another row of beach huts.

THE SITE: Just behind are the remains of part of the defences that linked in with the casino position. Several Tobruk emplacements and a long personnel bunker are visible. Having viewed these, move back along the beach to the inland bunker with the metal sculpture located in a small memorial garden.

This emplacement still has a steel cupola on top, which housed two machine guns able to fire in all directions through six openings. Alongside the bunker is a notice listing those of Kieffer's commandos who were killed on 6 June, some on the beach, some in the Boulevard Winston Churchill, some at the face of the casino. The commando lost 25 per cent of its effective strength during the attack. There are individually-named granite stones commemorating each of those killed on D-Day.

The steel cupola on top of one of the bunkers of the Riva Bella casino position, now used as a base for a memorial to the commandos. *(Author)*

Move on down the steps and turn left towards the casino, past the Hôtel St-George. Opposite the hotel is the *Musée No. 4 Commando* where you can find a complete description of the fighting in the area. One particularly interesting exhibit is the scale model of the casino strongpoint, which gives a good indication of the size and layout of its fortifications.

DIRECTIONS: After visiting the museum leave the car park, turn right and proceed along the Avenue du 6 Juin. About 300 metres down the road on the right is the *Musée le Mur de l'Atlantique*. There is a small car park in front of the museum and some parking places on the opposite side of the street.

Ouistreham Museums

Musée No. 4 Commando, Place Alfred Thomas, 14150 Ouistreham; tel: +33 (0)2 31 96 63 10. Open February to mid-November.

Musée le Mur de l'Atlantique, Le Bunker, Avenue du 6 Juin, 14150 Ouistreham; tel: +33 (0)2 31 97 28 69; fax: +33 (0)2 31 96 66 05; email: <bunkermusee@aol.com>. Open February to mid-November.

THE SITE: Outside the building are various exhibits relating to the war, including a German 88-mm gun and a V1 flying bomb. This is one of the best museums in the area, housed in a building that actually saw action during the invasion. The building was the control and observation tower for the area's coast defence guns. It stands over 17 metres high and has six floors, now all suitably restored and furnished with exhibition quality displays. The building was attacked by 4 Commando on D-Day, but the lightly weaponed troops were unable to get into the tower, so it was left for other units to deal with later.

The radio room of the German coastal observation post at Ouistreham recreated inside the Atlantic Wall Museum. *(Author)*

Major Murdoch McDougall, 4 Commando, attacked the control and observation tower.

'We swept around the corner, and my heart dropped to my boots. For there, beyond the ditch, tall, white and gleaming in the early morning sunlight, stood the tower, seemingly undamaged. Its completely blank face made it even more sinister. On our side there was no door, no window, just concrete. The only sign of life about it as we raced over the planks crossing the anti-tank ditch was the steady stream of stick-grenades that twitched and twirled over the parapet at the top.'

Source: Murdoch McDougall, *Swiftly They Struck*, p. 86.

Nothing was done about the control bunker until 9 June, when Lieutenant Bob Orrell, 91st Field Company, RE, visited the site. Orrell and his sappers blew open the main door and went inside. Then, from the upper chambers, they heard a voice calling: 'It's OK Tommy, we are coming out.' Fifty-two Germans surrendered to the young lieutenant.

DIRECTIONS: On leaving the museum, turn left towards the sea along Avenue de la Plage. At the end of the road, turn left and park.

THE SITE: Between here and the sea was where the 155-mm guns of the Ouistreham/Riva Bella battery had been (they were moved before D-Day). Walk onto the dunes to see the flat area where the guns were sited and to the left, in the middle of the go-kart track, the base of one of the emplacements can be seen.

This concrete base in the centre of a go-kart track is all that remains of the gun emplacements of the Riva Bella battery at Ouistreham. The position was attacked by 4 Commando on D-Day, but the guns had been moved inland a few weeks previously. *(Author)*

DIRECTIONS: Return to the car and head westwards along the road back towards the casino. At the roundabout, take the second exit along Boulevard Boivon Champeau and follow the road round to the left. The road marks the site of one arm of the wide anti-tank ditch that was dug to protect the landward approach to the seafront gun battery (*see picture on page 61*).

Proceed for about 600 metres to a pair of green gates on the right. This is now the entrance to a nursing home, which has been built onto an 18th-century redoubt originally forming part of the defences of the River Orne and the port of Ouistreham. This was one of the D-Day objectives of D Troop, 4 Commando.

Continue along to the end of the avenue and turn right to enter the complex of roads around the ferry port. Park in the car park in the centre of the road system on the left or drive round the road system and into the car park by the terminal building.

THE SITE: Close by is the lighthouse at Ouistreham and the lock gates at the start of the Orne Canal. When the men of 4 Commando arrived here on the afternoon of D-Day they found that the lock gates and the bridge were still held by the Germans. Their commanding officer, Lt-Col Robert Dawson, asked for armoured support and ten AVREs from 79th Assault Squadron came forward to help. The tanks enabled the western side of the canal to be taken, but the Germans blew the eastern span of the bridge and continued resistance. Infantry managed to get across the lock gates and, with the help of machine-gun and petard mortar fire from the tanks, cleared the Germans from the far side.

DIRECTIONS: Cross the road to the canal and walk across the lock in the direction of the lighthouse. Once over the canal, turn left and go about 300 metres towards the sea. Close by the harbour entrance is a bunker with a steel cupola on its roof. This was one of the defences guarding the canal entrance.

Visit the main ferry terminal at the Gare Maritime. Outside the entrance is a memorial to the men of the Royal Navy and Marines who crewed the armada of ships that took part in the invasion. The memorial was unveiled by Prince Philip in 2000.

THIS IS THE END OF THE TOUR: A meal or refreshments can now be taken in one of the many bars or restaurants lining the roads opposite the port.

Steel cupola mounted on top of a concrete bunker on the eastern side of the entrance to the Caen Canal at Ouistreham. *(Author)*

TOUR C

INLAND, THE EAST FLANK

OBJECTIVE: This tour traces the moves inland made by 2 E Yorks to its D-Day objectives and follows the route of Lord Lovat's 1st Special Service Brigade from Sword Beach to link up with Maj-Gen Gale's 6th Airborne Division on the River Orne.

DURATION/SUITABILITY: The distance covered is about 12 km; allow at least 2 hours to complete the tour. This tour is excellent for the cyclist, with good quiet roads over mostly flat open ground. It is equally good for the disabled with all major sites accessible by car.

DIRECTIONS: We start the tour as usual at the statue of Field Marshal Montgomery. Proceed south along the D60a towards Colleville-Montgomery. The village was renamed Colleville-Montgomery after the war by the local population in recognition of the part played by the field marshal during the liberation.

THE SITE: On both sides of the road are open fields and light woodland. This area was flooded before D-Day as part of the German defences and the British infantry had to move inland to

BATTLEFIELD TOURS

	Landing Zone W
ⓐ	Statue of FM Montgomery
ⓑ	Tobruk emplacement
ⓒ	Le Port church
ⓓ	Château de Bénouville
ⓔ	Pegasus Bridge
	Base map: IGN 1612OT

0   0.5   1

Kilometres

the right and left of the inundated ground. Even today the area is characterised by drainage ditches and at times by large areas of static water. After the lead companies of 2 E Yorks had got off the beach they moved along the road towards Ouistreham for a few hundred metres before moving south to their first objective, strongpoint Sole to the east of Colleville. Lovat's commandos exited the shoreline near to the site of Monty's statue, crossed the lateral road behind the beach (the D514) and moved over the ground close to the left of the D60a road. Their move was directed to the south-east to join up with 6th Airborne Division's landings on the bridges at Bénouville. 6 Commando led the advance; its brief was to move at speed, bypassing resistance posts if necessary and leaving them for the following commandos to deal with.

DIRECTIONS: Continue south along the D60a. After about 1.5 km, look to the right when approaching the entrance to the village of Colleville.

THE SITE: In the field, about 50 metres from the road, is a concrete defensive post of the so-called 'Tobruk' type. This weapons pit housed a machine gun or a mortar and was one of the two attacked by Lovat's commandos on their way through the area. It formed part of a local defensive position of trenches, wire and minefields covering the route inland from the sea. At the entrance to the village on the right is the French war memorial.

A derelict Tobruk emplacement near the road into Colleville from Sword Beach. This concrete weapons pit once formed part of the position guarding the northern entrance to the village and was captured by Lovat's commandos on their move to join up with the paratroopers across the River Orne. *(Author)*

DIRECTIONS: Turn left opposite the memorial along the D35a. Just after leaving the village, the road bends to the left and then right. Just after this second bend is an entrance to some farm buildings on the right.

THE SITE: The farm is built on the site of the underground headquarters of 1st Battalion, 736th Grenadier Regiment, code-named Sole by the Allies. The strongpoint was 2 E Yorks' first objective in its move inland from Sword Beach. The battalion attacked the position from across the road to the right in a set-piece operation that captured the strongpoint with little resistance. 2 E Yorks' next objective was strongpoint WN-12, the 155-mm battery code-named Daimler (held by 4th Battery, 1716th Artillery Regiment), which was about 1 km east of here.

DIRECTIONS: Continue along the road from the farm for 1.5 km to the outskirts of Ouistreham. At the roundabout take the first exit and drive along the D514 for a short distance towards the water tower. At the traffic lights, turn right into a small road leading up to the Stade Petit Bonheur. Drive to the end of the road and stop.

THE SITE: If you look to the left across the field you may be able to see two of the concrete casemates that held the guns of strongpoint Daimler some 250 metres south-southeast. (If your visit is taken in late summer or early autumn, this view may be obscured by crops growing in the field.)

The view from the north of two of the casemates of battery Daimler, which was taken by 2 E Yorks on D-Day. The battalion's other objective was the nearby headquarters at Sole, located 1 km away to the north-west. *(Author)*

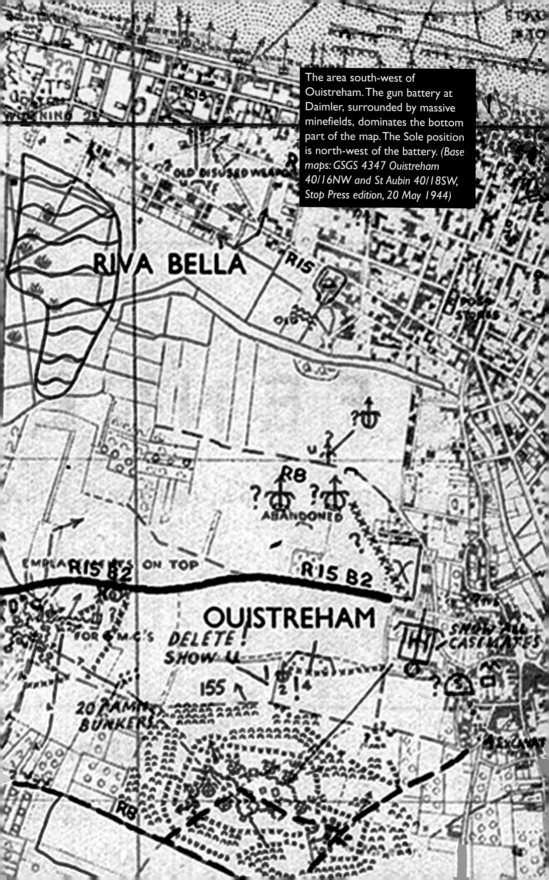

The area south-west of Ouistreham. The gun battery at Daimler, surrounded by massive minefields, dominates the bottom part of the map. The Sole position is north-west of the battery. (Base maps: GSGS 4347 Ouistreham 40/16NW and St Aubin 40/18SW, Stop Press edition, 20 May 1944)

DIRECTIONS: Go back to the traffic lights and turn right along the D514, heading towards the water tower again. At the roundabout a short distance along the road, turn right taking the first exit, signposted to St-Aubin-d'Arquenay. At this point, if you look carefully, several of the bunkers of the Daimler battery can now be seen on the right within some private grounds.

To make a closer inspection of the Daimler site, proceed for around 200 metres from the roundabout and then turn right into a small rough track (the Chemin des Pelerins). Go along this for 200 metres to the end of a high hedge. Turn right here and continue for 300 metres along a dirt track towards a large area of undergrowth. This track may not be passable in wet weather.

THE SITE: On the left in the middle of the field can be seen a Tobruk emplacement which

The silted-up embrasure of one of Daimler's gun emplacements. *(Author)*

formed part of the outer defences of the strongpoint. At the end of the track you are well within the Daimler fortified area. Two of the gun casemates are accessible to the intrepid explorer in the thick undergrowth. In the surrounding fields are a few more concrete remains of the battery's outer fortifications. 2 E Yorks took this gun battery during the afternoon of D-Day after a bombardment by 76th Field Regiment, supported by the guns of the tanks of 13th/18th Hussars.

DIRECTIONS: Return to the metalled road and turn left to continue on to St-Aubin-d'Arquenay. The great open area to the left was the landing site for 6th Airborne Division's follow-up glider force on D-Day evening. Drive along into the village until the road junction signed to Bénouville and Caen; turn left here to join the D35.

THE SITE: The first troops to arrive in St-Aubin were the men of 6 Commando, who passed through the village in the late morning. The commandos met some spirited resistance in St-Aubin, for the village contained two resistance posts, WN-15

One of the now overgrown casemates of battery Daimler. The position was manned on D-Day by 4th Battery, 1716th Artillery Regiment. *(Author)*

and WN-15a. Allied aircraft and warships had attacked both these fortifications during the early morning and the village had suffered some destruction. 6 Commando pressed on with some speed, passing quickly through the built-up area to join with the airborne division over the Orne and leaving the rest of Lovat's brigade to clear the remaining Germans from St-Aubin.

> **Brigadier Lord Lovat, 1st Special Service Brigade, recalled meeting a group of German troops as he and his men approached St-Aubin-d'Arquenay.**
>
> 'The enemy – a platoon about thirty strong – looked a soft touch; the sun was in their eyes and we were unobserved. I made a quick decision to ambush them. The fire order that was whispered down to the ambushing party is not found in training manuals: "Pick the officers and NCOs and let them come right in." The ragged volley caused a surprise: dust flew off the back of the fair haired platoon commander as he spun round and fell; half-a-dozen others who had bunched in the centre on reaching the buildings went down in a heap. The rest took cover in the corn.'
> *Source:* Lord Lovat, *March Past*, p. 320.

DIRECTIONS: Leave the village by the D35 and move out into the open ground to the south-east. On the right is the ground over which the main body of 1 Norfolks advanced to its D-Day objective Rover, the hill-top farm of Bellevue 2 km to the west in front of a line of trees marking the skyline beyond. On the left is one of 6th Airborne Division's landing zones. This great expanse of open ground was LZ W and it stretched from just south of Ouistreham to this road.

THE SITE: During the early hours of D-Day, two brigades of 6th Airborne Division had been dropped by parachute or landed in gliders on the other side of the Orne valley to seize the bridges over the River Orne and the Orne Canal at Bénouville and to carve out a lodgement on the left flank of the invasion area to protect the seaborne landings on Sword Beach. There were too few aircraft available to carry the whole of the division in one lift, so the third brigade of Maj-Gen Gale's division landed here in gliders during the evening of 6 June. This later airborne landing was called Operation 'Mallard' and it was the first daylight glider operation of any magnitude to be made during the war. A total of 248 gliders successfully touched down on LZ W and on LZ N over the Orne at Ranville, bringing 6th Airlanding Brigade, the Airborne Armoured Reconnaissance Regiment and 211th Light Battery, Royal Artillery, to complete the division, together with supplies of ammunition and stores.

DIRECTIONS: Continue along the D35 to the road junction on the hill, bear to the left and pass down underneath the dual carriageway which links Ouistreham and Caen. Continue to the small roundabout and take the first exit on the right.

THE SITE: This is the village of le Port. In the early hours of 6 June 1944 it marked the northern edge of 6th Airborne Division's lodgement around the bridges over the River Orne and the canal. The bridges had been captured by Major John Howard's D Company of 2nd Battalion, The Oxfordshire and Buckinghamshire Light Infantry, in a brilliant *coup de main*. Howard's men landed in three gliders, which touched down just metres from the canal bridge, to the complete surprise of the garrison. Both bridges were then captured intact and held against repeated counter-attacks. This small assault force continued in control of the vital bridges until reinforced later by 7th Parachute Battalion. These fresh paratroops expanded Howard's small lodgement and took control of the villages of Bénouville and le Port on the western side of the canal. The Germans counter-attacked this small force again and again throughout the remainder of the night and into the daylight hours.

The canal bridge at Bénouville was captured by Major Howard's company of 2nd Oxford and Bucks Light Infantry during the first minutes of D-Day. This is the original bridge, which was removed to the nearby *Mémorial Pegasus* museum when it was replaced by a more modern structure in 1994. *(Author)*

Alongside the small church in le Port is the spot where Captain Richard Todd, later famous as a film actor, had his slit trench. Todd was serving with 7th Parachute Battalion and dropped by parachute with his unit during the early hours of 6 June. He returned to this area again in the early 1960s to play the part of Major Howard in the film *The Longest Day*. In the churchyard are a number of Commonwealth war graves, mostly of airborne troops killed during the first few days of the invasion.

DIRECTIONS: At the next roundabout take the second exit, leading into Bénouville.

THE SITE: This road was the route taken by 2 Warwicks from 185th Infantry Brigade late on D-Day. It was also the road down which most of the German counter-attacks were directed.

Colonel Hans von Luck's 125th Panzergrenadier Regiment supported the German counter-attack.

'In the late afternoon, almost the same time as the armoured group west of the Orne, we set off. Our goal: to push through to Ranville and the two Orne bridges. The reconnaissance battalion went straight into the attack from its march and, supported by the panzer company, surprised their opponents. Then all hell broke loose. The heaviest naval guns, up to 38 cm in calibre, artillery and fighter-bombers plastered us without pause. Radio contact was lost, wounded came back, and the men of the reconnaissance battalion were forced to take cover. I had gone up with the attack and saw the disaster. I managed to run forward to the commander of the battalion and gave him fresh orders to break off the attack at once and take up defensive positions.'

Source: Hans von Luck, *Panzer Commander*, p. 179.

This area to the west of the Orne Canal continued to attract the attention of German forces coming up from the south. By mid-afternoon on D-Day the position was thought to be in great danger and so 2 Warwicks was sent across to push back the panzergrenadiers. 9th Infantry Brigade also sent 1 KOSB to St-Aubin-d'Arquenay, to act as a backstop in the event of a German breakthrough at Bénouville.

DIRECTIONS: Continue for about 1 km. On the left behind the stone wall are the grounds of the Château de Bénouville.

THE SITE: 2 Warwicks advanced through here and along the path by the canal with the support of a few tanks from 13th/18th Hussars. The Germans were quite well established around this southern part of Bénouville and it took until dark for the battalion to advance as far as the outskirts of Blainville.

DIRECTIONS: Continue to the roundabout. Blainville is 1 km ahead of this point and this was roughly the furthest point reached by the main body of 2 Warwicks on D-Day. Go right round the roundabout and return to the centre of Bénouville. At the next roundabout, turn right towards Ranville on the D514. Go down towards the canal bridge and pull over where safe.

Commonwealth graves by the church at le Port close by the Orne Canal. 23 burials of men from the 6th Airborne Division, including that of one of its chaplains, lie amongst French civilian graves. *(Author)*

THE SITE: Lovat's 1st Special Service Brigade advanced down this road to join up with the paratroopers at Pegasus Bridge in the early afternoon of D-Day. Then Maj-Gen Gale sent three of its commandos across the Orne up to the northern edge of the lodgement near Sallenelles and the fourth, 3 Commando, to reinforce his paratroopers in the south of the lodgement near Ranville.

DIRECTIONS: Walk down to the canal. Just before the bridge on the right is the famous *Café Gondrée*, supposedly the first house to be liberated in France during the first minutes of D-Day.

On the opposite side of the road is a Centaur tank, which touched down on Sword Beach with 5th Battery, Royal Marine Armoured Support Group. Cross the bridge and then turn right.

THE SITE: Maj Howard's three gliders landed close by here at 0016 hours on 6 June 1944, heralding the start of the invasion. His men leapt from their gliders and seized the canal bridge from the German garrison before it could be blown. The bridge then came to be known as Pegasus Bridge, after the emblem of British airborne forces. The original bridge has now been removed and a larger structure, more able to carry today's traffic, has been installed in its place. However, the original is not far away, for it now rests just a short distance along the road to the right in the grounds of the *Mémorial Pegasus* museum. The anti-tank gun in a pit by the bridge is original, although it was slightly re-sited during the replacement of the canal bridge.

THIS IS THE END OF THE TOUR: The bridge is part of the D514 road so returning to the start of the tour is simple. Before doing so tourers may wish to pay a visit to the museum to find out more about the actions fought by the airborne troops and then take lunch or tea at the nearby *Café Gondrée*. These actions and other sites in this locality are also more fully described in the companion volume Battle Zone Normandy *Orne Bridgehead*.

The *Café Gondrée* on the western side of the Orne Canal, the first house to be liberated during the invasion. *(Author)*

TOUR D

THE DRIVE ON CAEN

OBJECTIVE: This tour follows the route inland made by 1 S Lancs to Hermanville and then traces the drive towards Caen undertaken by 185th Infantry Brigade's armoured column of 2 KSLI and the supporting tanks of the Staffordshire Yeomanry.

DURATION/SUITABILITY: This tour covers some 14 km; allow at least 2 hours. This is again a good tour for the cyclist, but there are some hills and busy roads towards the end of the tour. For the disabled, all major sites are accessible by car

DIRECTIONS: Begin at Monty's statue as before. Go west along the D514 towards Lion-sur-Mer to the second set of traffic lights. The pedestrianised road on the right leads to one of the main exits from Sword Beach. Turn left along the D60b, named Rue de 6 Juin, towards the main village of Hermanville-sur-Mer.

One of the main exits from Sword Beach at the junction of Place du Cuirassé Courbet and the road to Hermanville. *(Author)*

THE SITE: This was the route taken inland just after the landings by 1 S Lancs and by most battalions of the follow-up brigades. It was the main route southwards from Sword Beach and led towards the strategically important high ground of

BATTLEFIELD TOURS

Périers Ridge and thence to Caen. In 1944 the ground on either side was open; the new housing estates on the right are modern. On the left the ground was flooded and marshy, forcing all tanks and vehicles to use this road to get south through Hermanville. Not surprisingly, huge traffic jams built up along here and on the lateral roads behind the beach as hundreds of men and numerous vehicles all tried to leave the beaches.

Once 1 S Lancs had got off the beach at around 0830 hours, the battalion found little opposition in its way. Most of the resistance was grouped around strongpoints on the right and left flanks. B and D Companies of 1 S Lancs moved down this road and entered Hermanville, quickly followed by battalion headquarters and C Company. The remaining company, A, moved along further to the right and became embroiled in the fighting to clear Lion-sur-Mer alongside 41 RM Commando. By 0900 hours Hermanville had been taken and the troops of 1 S Lancs had consolidated their hold on the village, with battalion headquarters set up in the grounds of the church. The early capture of Hermanville enabled the incoming troops of the

Troops moving inland through Hermanville past the French war memorial close by the church. *(IWM B5018)*

follow-up battalions to pass through and fan out into the open countryside to the south.

DIRECTIONS: Proceed to the next junction and turn left to join the D60 into the town. Carry on to the stop sign by the church in the centre of Hermanville.

THE SITE: Opposite the church on the side of the car park is a sign commemorating the site of the well that supplied fresh water each day for the invading forces. All local supplies of water feeding the Germans and the local French population were from concrete water towers with electrically driven pumps, generally drawing water from narrow-bore wells. All of these were put out of action when the power supply from Caen failed. On the evening of 6 June, a water-point was set up here and eventually there were 30 taps lined up along the wall supplying over seven million litres of water in the first three weeks after the landings.

DIRECTIONS: Continue into the town, passing by the French war memorial on the right. Immediately after the memorial is a set of metal gates at the entrance to the Château de Hermanville, which is now the *mairie*. Park in the parking area opposite.

The gates of the *mairie* at Hermanville, once the entrance to the town's château. (*Author*)

THE SITE: The château was taken over on D-Day by Maj-Gen Rennie as his divisional headquarters. Twelve field hospitals were later established here in the grounds and in the nearby fields, all of which continued to deal with casualties until the fighting had moved out of the Normandy region. There is a plaque on the gatepost to commemorate the château's use as British 3rd Infantry Division's command post.

DIRECTIONS: Return to your car and continue along the D60, up the hill and through the village, towards a set of road

Sword Beach

Lion-sur-Mer
le Bas Lion

la Brèche d'Hermanville
Colleville-
-Montgomery Plage

a

**Hermanville-
-sur-Mer**

b
d **c**

OUISTREHAM

WN-18
(MORRIS)

**Colleville-
Montgomery**

P É R I E R S

WN-17
(HILLMAN)

POINT 61

St-Aubin-d'Arquenay

R I D G E

ROVER

Périers-sur-le-Dan

e

Bénouville

Commune

f

de Biéville-Beuville

g

Biéville

Blainville-sur-Orne

h

a Statue of FM Montgomery

b Hermanville church

c Site of D-Day well

d Château de Hermanville

e Crossing point over River le Dan

f Beuville church

g Château de Biéville

h Natural anti-tank feature

Base map: IGN 1612OT

**HÉROUVILLE-
ST-CLAIR**

**LÉBISEY
WOOD**

0   0.5   1
Kilometres

junctions. This is the route taken by 185th Infantry Brigade on its drive to Caen. Go past the first turning (the D35 to Colleville) and continue to the junction immediately after it. Turn left here onto the D60 towards Périers-sur-le-Dan and Biéville.

THE SITE: Just out of Hermanville the road bends to the right. If you look to the left a group of trees marks the site of the battery at strongpoint Morris, captured by 1 Suffolks at about 1300 hours on 6 June. The road now climbs up onto the eastern edge of Périers Ridge with open ground on both sides. This ridge should have been captured by the time that 185th Infantry Brigade had begun its advance on Caen, but the battalion allocated to this task, 1 Suffolks, was still trying to get past the strongpoints of Morris and Hillman south of Colleville when 2 KSLI began its move.

> **Major G.L.Y. Radcliffe, adjutant 2 KSLI, recalled the storm of fire sweeping the high ground south of Hermanville.**
>
> 'It was clear that this ridge had not yet been captured by 8th Infantry Brigade. The enemy opened both small arms and mortar fire on X Company as they moved up the slope and held them up. The commanding officer, therefore, ordered W Company to outflank this post. When the battalion first came under fire on this slope everyone instinctively went to ground. A brother officer has related to me, how looking round, and feeling extremely frightened, he saw Colonel Maurice walking up the centre of the road, playing with the chin-strap of his helmet as he always did. He thought, "Well – if he is all right I suppose I shall be too," and got up. This was typical of the complete disregard of enemy fire which Colonel Maurice always showed. The example spread and in a few minutes the men were moving forward steadily.'
>
> *Source:* G.L.Y. Radcliffe, *The King's Shropshire Light Infantry*, p. 14.

This area of open ground was also used as an assembly area for 9th Infantry Brigade after its battalions had landed. For the few weeks following the landings it was also the rear area for many units being pulled out of the line. 2 KSLI advanced along this route on its move to Caen. It was along this stretch of the

The southern slopes of Périers Ridge along the road from Hermanville to Caen, which formed the axis of the advance made by 185th Infantry Brigade on 6 June. At the bottom of the hill is the diminutive River le Dan, with the two villages of Beuville and Biéville in the centre left of the picture. The wooded slopes of Lébisey and the city of Caen can be seen along the left skyline. *(Author)*

road that the tanks of the Staffordshire Yeomanry caught up with the battalion advancing on foot and gave the infantry armoured support. C Squadron, Staffordshire Yeomanry, continued with 2 KSLI while B Squadron deployed on the ground to the right, where it lost five of its tanks to an 88-mm gun firing from the crest of the ridge.

DIRECTIONS: At the top of the hill is a crossroads where the road from Colleville joins from the left and the road down to Périers on the right. Carry on over the crossroads and stop when safe to do so.

THE SITE: This area was known as Point 61 in 1944, although the crest is shown on modern maps as being 58 metres above sea level. This is the highest point on the ridge and was a very important site, giving a panoramic view of the whole region.

A strongpoint near here on the road down to Périers-sur-le-Dan contained a German field battery. The Germans here fired on the flanks of 2 KSLI's advance and prevented the supporting tanks from advancing. Lt-Col Maurice of 2 KSLI detached Z Company to deal with the position.

From the top of the ridge, Caen can be clearly seen ahead away to the south. To the rear, looking north is a commanding view of Sword Beach. To the west is Périers-sur-le-Dan and to the east are Hillman and the village of St-Aubin-d'Arquenay. German observers based at this point were able to direct artillery fire onto the whole length of the landing beaches and assembly areas.

DIRECTIONS: Proceed along the D60 across the plateau and down towards the village of Beuville.

THE SITE: On either side of the road is open countryside. Away over on the left is the ground that 1 Norfolks advanced across on its move inland, while the area to the immediate right and also beyond Périers was the route that 21st Panzer Division took on its counter-attack towards the sea. On D-Day, the tanks of the Staffordshire Yeomanry were in this area and the panzers drove right across their front.

> **Sergeant Joyce, A Squadron, Staffordshire Yeomanry, remembered 21st Panzer Division's counter-attack.**
>
> 'I was moving my Sherman into very good cover on the right of the squadron overlooking an open piece of ground between two wooded areas, when I was amazed to find some enemy tanks moving in line ahead across my front at a range of only 600 yards. I allowed the armour to come well into the open and fired on the last tank, scoring a direct hit with the first shot. I then traversed down the line of tanks, knocking out two with three shots and finally finished off the fourth tank, leaving them all burning wrecks. Two others which escaped came under fire from B Squadron.'
>
> Source: D.F. Underhill, *The Queen's Own Royal Staffordshire Yeomanry in World War II*, p. 26.

Ahead are the two villages of Beuville and Biéville, with the tree-lined slopes of the Lébisey Ridge beyond. Lt-Col Maurice placed the supporting guns of 41st Anti-tank Battery along the southern slopes to the right, to protect his flanks.

BATTLEFIELD TOURS

DIRECTIONS: As you continue down the hill another road from Périers-sur-le-Dan joins from the right and a little distance further on the road crosses the small River le Dan.

THE SITE: Lt-Col Maurice stopped his force near here because of small arms fire from the village and sent two companies forward onto the open ground on the right to leapfrog past the villages and get behind the Germans in Beuville and Biéville. The rest of his group, with tanks in support, moved on by the road.

DIRECTIONS: Care needs to be taken passing through the centre of the next two villages as the road priority changes, giving right of way to traffic entering from the right. The area can also be quite busy in rush hour periods.

Proceed along the road through Beuville, passing the church. Head through the centre and up the hill, passing some post-war houses. Go across the modern traffic lights, then out of Beuville into the older part of the village of Biéville. On the right are the big gates that lead into the courtyard of the château. This was the scene of some fierce fighting by 2 KSLI when clearing the village.

Continue past a modern development on the left, then a few old houses on the right and out of the village. Some 400 metres south of the village the road descends into a steep gully, which formed a natural anti-tank obstacle across the line of 185th Infantry Brigade's advance. Going down the hill, there is a monument on the right. Park opposite on the left in a small parking area.

THE SITE: The monument is to 'Peace and Liberty' and commemorates the battles fought in this vicinity. The tiny valley marks the front line for the four weeks following D-Day. Y Company of 2 KSLI and some tanks got across this feature and up into the woods and village of Lébisey on 6 June, but had to retreat after being counter-attacked by panzergrenadiers from GenMaj Feuchtinger's 21st Panzer Division. Further attacks by 2 Warwicks and 1 Norfolks the next day also ended in failure and this sector of the line became static whilst British 3rd Infantry Division attacked towards Caen elsewhere.

DIRECTIONS: Return to your car and carry on along the road across the ditch and up the hill. There is open countryside on both sides with Lébisey Wood running across the top of the ridge.

THE SITE: 2 Warwicks' and 1 Norfolks' attacks on 7 June traversed the open ground to the left, up the slopes and into the wood along the top. The D60 road followed by the tour was the route taken during the attack by 2 Warwicks' carriers and anti-tank guns, led by Lieutenant Bannerman, when they tried to meet up with their besieged comrades in Lébisey Wood. Five of the carriers were knocked out while coming up this hill. Bannerman's vehicle managed to carry on through the German positions on the top and out onto the plateau that leads to Caen just 4 km away. Here it was destroyed and Bannerman and his men captured.

DIRECTIONS: Towards the top of the hill there is a good deal of modern housing on the right covering the forward edge of the ridge. The road rises to a set of traffic lights. Turn left towards Hérouville-St-Clair on the D226b and pull over where it is safe to do so. This road runs along the face of Lébisey Wood which is on the right. Behind, back at the traffic lights, the road is named the Rue de la 3ème Division, and leads into the old village of Lébisey. Since the war the village has been swallowed up by new development. The western part of the ridge from which 21st Panzer Division launched its attack is now completely covered by houses and the woods in front of the village have mostly gone.

The deep ditch which formed a natural anti-tank barrier across the road to Caen between Biéville and Lébisey. The view is looking eastwards with the slopes of the Lébisey Ridge rising to the right. *(Author)*

BATTLEFIELD TOURS

THE SITE: GenMaj Feuchtinger assembled the tanks of Colonel von Oppeln's 100th/22nd Panzer Regiment in the area north of, and to the west of, Lébisey. Colonel Rauch gathered his 192nd Panzergrenadier Regiment further west, closer to Épron and Cambes. On the right is the edge of Lébisey Wood, which 1 Norfolks and 2 Warwicks penetrated on 7 June but could not take. On the left is the ground over which they attacked.

THIS IS THE END OF THE TOUR: Continue along the road to the Ouistreham–Caen dual carriageway, the D515, and follow the signs to Ouistreham to returning to the starting point.

TOUR E

MORRIS, HILLMAN AND ROVER

OBJECTIVE: This tour follows the route of 1 Suffolks from Sword Beach to Colleville and the capture of strongpoints Morris and Hillman. It continues with 1 Norfolks' advance to Rover and 2 Warwicks' activity to the left of the beachhead.

DURATION/SUITABILITY: The tour covers some 13.5 km and will probably take about 3 hours by car. For the cyclist there are good quiet roads, but it includes some long hills towards the end of the tour. This is also a good tour for the disabled; all major sites are visible from the car, but there is no disabled access to the bunkers at Hillman.

DIRECTIONS: Begin at Monty's statue and head west along the D514 towards Lion-sur-Mer. At the first set of traffic lights turn left along the Boulevard de la 3ème Division Britannique, following signs to the War Graves Commission Cemetery.

THE SITE: 1 Suffolks, 8th Infantry Brigade's follow-up battalion, landed after the assault battalions and left Queen Beach near the start of this road. A short distance away on the

The Commonwealth War Graves Commission cemetery at Hermanville, where many of the men who were killed on D-Day are buried. *(Author)*

left is a memorial to the commander of the French battleship *Courbet*, Admiral Wietzel. The *Courbet* was sunk off Sword Beach a few days after the assault to form part of the Gooseberry breakwater protecting the landing beaches. On the right opposite the monument was 1 Suffolks' intended assembly area. The men of the battalion were meant to have formed up in the small wood here, but when they arrived they found that the Germans had chopped it down and used the timber as stakes. The wooden poles, known to the German troops as 'Rommel's Asparagus', were planted upright in the surrounding fields to prevent the ground being used as landing zones for gliders.

The wood on the right after a few hundred metres where the road bends to the right was 1 Suffolks' actual assembly area. It was here that the battalion commander, Lt-Col Goodwin, gathered his men and organised the advance to the strongpoints of Morris and Hillman at Colleville. 1 Suffolks was joined by a troop of 13th/18th Hussars Sherman tanks for the attack. They moved off in the mid-morning, crossed the road near here and then moved parallel to it for around 600 metres, before striking out towards the south-east across the fields towards Colleville.

DIRECTIONS: Continue down the road past the holiday parks until the sharp right hand bend. Turn left and park; the war cemetery is now on the right.

BATTLEFIELD TOURS

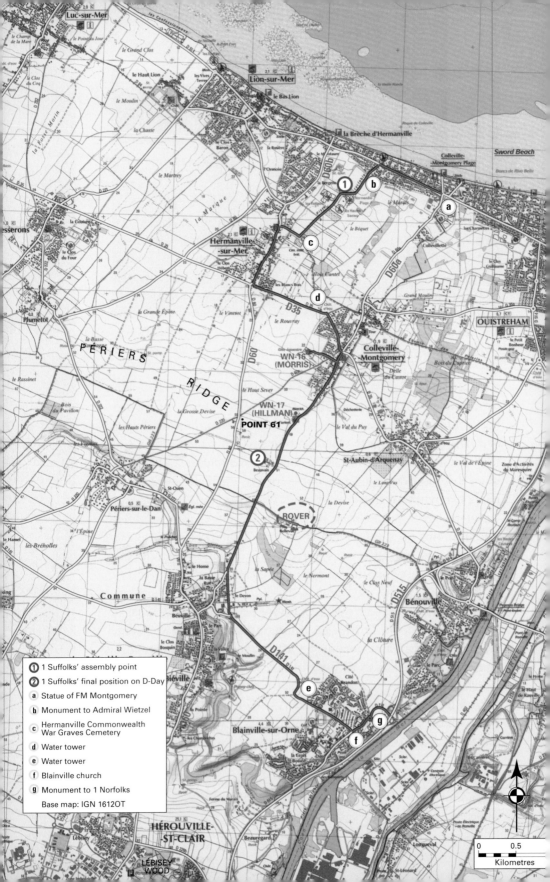

Luc-sur-Mer

le Champ
de la Mare

le Point du Jour

le Grand Clos

les Vives Terres

Lion-sur-Mer

le Bas Lion

la Brèche d'Hermanville

Sword Beach

Colleville-
Montgomery Plage

a

le Haut Lion

la Chasse

le Clos
du Coq

le Moulin

le Martray

le Clos
Baron

l'Ormoie

b

le Marais

le Béquet

Colleville

les Charmettes

Collevillette

le Clos
Guillaume

Hermanville-
-sur-Mer

c

le Clos
Hébert

Cim. mon.
brit.

Bois Cantel

les Blancs Bois

le Rouvray

le Vinetot

d

D35

Grand Moulin

OUISTREHAM

Plumetot

PÉRIERS

la Basse

Bois
du Pavillon

la Grande Épine

le Haut Sever

WN-16
(MORRIS)

D60

RIDGE

la Grosse Devise

les Hauts Périers

WN-17
(HILLMAN)

POINT 61

Colleville-
Montgomery

le Val du Puy

Déchetterie

Bois du Caprice

le Rassinet

les Lignots

St-Aubin-d'Arquenay

le Val de l'Épine

Zone d'Activités
du Maresquier

②

Beauvais

la Devise

ROVER

Périers-sur-le-Dan

St-Ouen

le Longueras

le Nermont

le Clos Neuf

Bénouville

Commune

Beuville

le Home
la Basse
Rue

la Sapée

le Devon

le Clos
Bosquin

le Clos
du Parc

D141

la Clôture

le Parc

le Home
le Val de Ranville

e

Blainville-sur-Orne

f

g

Cité
Beaudon

les Churchottes

**HÉROUVILLE-
ST-CLAIR**

LÉBISEY
WOOD

---

①	1 Suffolks' assembly point
②	1 Suffolks' final position on D-Day
a	Statue of FM Montgomery
b	Monument to Admiral Wietzel
c	Hermanville Commonwealth War Graves Cemetery
d	Water tower
e	Water tower
f	Blainville church
g	Monument to 1 Norfolks
	Base map: IGN 1612OT

0   0.5

Kilometres

THE SITE: The Commonwealth War Cemetery at Hermanville contains the graves of 1,005 men, many of whom were killed on D-Day. There are 986 British, 13 Canadian, three Australian and three French burials in the cemetery.

DIRECTIONS: Return to your car and continue along the road to Hermanville a short distance away. Follow the road round to the left and drive up the Grand Rue through the village and past the church and château in the direction of Périers. At the top of the hill a few metres before the main junction turn left onto the D35 to Colleville-Montgomery. Go on for a few hundred metres.

THE SITE: To the left is the ground that 1 Suffolks crossed on the move inland. The battalion passed to the north of the water tower into the northern end of Colleville, together with the accompanying tanks. To the right, about 750 metres away, the line of trees marks the location of the gun battery at Morris.

DIRECTIONS: Take the turning on the right just after the water tower and go into the centre of Colleville. Stop at the crossroads and turn right, heading towards Caen. After about 100 metres look for the sign to Caen and turn next right after 100 metres more onto the Rue de Caen. Go over the next small crossroads immediately ahead and, as the road swings to the left, take the smaller road which leads straight on. Continue for a short distance until the road turns to the right into a modern housing estate. Straight ahead is a small track, which looks like a private drive but is not. Motor a short distance along the track and park.

THE SITE: You are now within what were the wired and mined outer fortifications of Morris. To your left is a private riding school, with the casemates of the Morris battery now located in its grounds. The area to your right was open fields in 1944.

After clearing the village of any enemy, B Company of 1 Suffolks moved up to a point near here where its men could overlook the outer wire of the battery, ready to launch a set-piece attack. The company opened its attack by directing a few rounds of ranging fire from the field guns in the rear, prior to the infantry blowing a gap through the outer wire. These first few shells alone were enough to convince the 67 men of the garrison that it was better to surrender. They had already endured bombing raids and heavy shelling from warships that day and had had enough. Morris was then occupied without loss.

DIRECTIONS: By walking a little further down the track it is possible to see two of the strongpoint's concrete gun emplacements behind the trees. Return to the car and go back towards Colleville village. In the field on the right is a small bunker, which was part of the strongpoint's outer defences.

One of the reinforced-concrete gun casemates of the Morris gun battery at Colleville, captured by B Company, 1 Suffolks, during the early afternoon of D-Day. *(Author)*

At the Rue de Caen bear left and go back over the crossroads to the junction in the village. Turn right, away from the centre of Colleville, and proceed up the hill towards Beuville. About half a kilometre along what is now called Rue du Suffolk Régiment, the road becomes a sunken lane with high banks. A little way further up the road on the right is a signpost for the Hillman Fortification. Park in the small space in front of a large bunker.

THE SITE: The road from Colleville to here was the main route up to the fortified area and was used, along with a parallel track 100 metres on the right, as the axis for 1 Suffolks' first attack. Almost the whole of Hillman was underground, with only the two steel cupolas on top of their bunkers visible to the attackers.

The large bunker beside the parking area, once part of the Hillman complex, and the plot of land on which it stands were

Driver Turnham hangs out his washing on a makeshift line at the rear of one of the casemates of strongpoint Morris after the battery had been captured by 1 Suffolks. *(IWM B5876)*

given to the Suffolk Regiment by the landowner, Madame Lenauld, in 1989 as a permanent memorial to the men of 1st Battalion. Since then the local commune of Colleville-Montgomery has formed a society, Les Amis du Suffolk Régiment, which has looked after the whole site. Over the past few years, local people have gradually renovated the blockhouses and made the fortifications accessible to visitors. The main Suffolk bunker by the car park has two plaques fixed to its walls. The first is a memorial to the men of the Suffolk Regiment who fell during the fighting on 6 June 1944 and those who later died during the liberation of Europe. The other plaque has a description of the fortification and how it was captured. On top of the bunker is a large orientation map.

The site at Hillman often has visitor days at weekends in summer, when some of the emplacements are opened to the

The 1 Suffolks memorial bunker at strongpoint Hillman outside Colleville. The building was the transport and storage site for the German position. *(Author)*

public by the society, most notably during several weekends in July and August. It also normally has guided tours on Tuesdays in June, July and August. Before visiting, please check first with one of the local tourist offices that this continues to be the case. Points of interest include the Suffolk bunker with its small exhibition and Colonel Krug's regimental command bunker. English-speaking guides are sometimes available to give help.

Hillman is one of the most important and satisfying D-Day locations to visit, for it is still possible to walk the battlefield and recreate in your mind's eye the events on the very spot that they happened 60 years ago. After the war the area was cleared for agricultural use and the bunkers and emplacements covered with earth and rubble, which preserved them in good condition. Subsequent excavations have restored them to their wartime state. The Hillman fortifications have much to offer the visitor at any time of the year, even on days when the bunkers are not open, for each significant spot now has an information stand alongside it explaining its use, location and capture.

On the northern edge of the site is the large concrete shelter which housed the headquarters of Colonel Krug's 736th Grenadier Regiment. A plaque on the wall recalls its eventual capture and the nearby information stand describes its interior. The entrance to the blockhouse is covered by weapon slits and an open Tobruk machine-gun post on its roof. Inside can be seen the range and bearing indicators painted on its inner side. A short distance away is one of the distinctive steel cupolas which housed two machine guns. Access to this was from inside the headquarters bunker. These armoured structures were impervious even to point-blank fire from tanks and their weapons proved to be most troublesome and costly to 1 Suffolks during its attacks.

Now stand with the cupola behind you and look towards the village. The assaulting companies of 1 Suffolks attacked Hillman from this direction, penetrating through the belts of wire and the minefield between them. They got into the trenches behind the second belt of wire only to find that most of the defenders had disappeared into the concrete bunkers. Machine-gun and small arms fire swept the whole of the complex, confining the attacking infantry to the trenches that they had managed to capture.

Corporal Rayson, 1 Suffolks, took part in the attack on Hillman.

'We crawled through a field of barley and waited till the engineers lifted some mines and taped a track through the minefield. Another party got rid of the wire with Bangalore torpedoes. Then we went in. The first two through, a corporal and a private, were killed as soon as they got through the gap. A machine gun in a tank turret was mounted right in front of the gap. We all got down and he kept us down. Bullets whizzed above our heads. One hit the pick axe on my back, one went through my gas cape rolled up on my belt.'

Source: Robin Neillands and Roderick de Normann, *D-Day 1944*, p. 284.

A further attack, supported by tanks, was more successful and 1 Suffolks gradually cleared each bunker. However, it was not until next morning that Colonel Krug surrendered himself.

DIRECTIONS: Return to your car. Continue along the road away from Colleville village for about 300 metres and stop.

BATTLEFIELD TOURS

The communications room inside the command bunker of 736th Grenadier Regiment at the Hillman position. *(Author)*

Entrance to one of the great bunkers of strongpoint Hillman. Access to the entrance is covered by the machine-gun aperture straight ahead. The two round openings on the wall to the right that look like ventilation embrasures are linked together as a booby trap. Any grenade inserted through the hole at the top will fall out of the hole at the bottom at the feet of the attacker. *(Author)*

This machine-gun aperture inside one of the bunkers of the Hillman complex covered the approach to the entrance to the emplacement. *(Author)*

THE SITE: The route of the advance made by two of the battalions of 185th Infantry Brigade is over to the left. Two companies of 1 Norfolks crossed the wide-open fields closest to you on their move towards the battalion's intermediate objective, strongpoint Rover. This was based around Bellevue Farm, which the men of the battalion eventually called Norfolk House, and it can now be seen as the prominent range of buildings along the ridge some 800 metres ahead and to the left.

1 Norfolks was supposed to be part of 185th Infantry Brigade's rapid advance on Caen, but it had been unable to get past Colleville to Rover because 1 Suffolks had not taken Hillman. By mid-afternoon, 1 Norfolks' commanding officer had decided not to wait for Hillman to be captured, but to press on with two companies directly across the fields from Colleville towards Rover. The remainder of the battalion went *via* the village of St-Aubin-d'Arquenay.

The nearest two companies of 1 Norfolks made their advance a few hundred metres from the road the tour has just moved up. While they were crossing this open ground they came under accurate fire from the guns of the Hillman strongpoint. The infantry were pinned down for 2½ hours in the fields, with no cover at all, unable to move. During this advance they suffered over 40 casualties, 14 of whom were killed. This was more than 1 Suffolks experienced in capturing the strongpoint at Hillman.

Private W. Evans, B Company, 1 Norfolks, participated in the attack on Rover.

'We had covered two or three miles and were doing well until we came to a cornfield. Then Jerry machine guns in a small pillbox opened up. The lads were soon being cut to pieces as the machine guns with their tremendous rate of fire scythed through the three-foot high golden corn. I remember one of the company cooks behind me getting a bullet in his neck. That was the day I first saw the red poppies in France in the cornfields, diving to the ground out of the machine gun fire. My nose was stuck right amongst them! They reminded me of the hell and horrors of the 1914 war which my father had talked so often about.'

Source: John Lincoln, *Thank God and the Infantry*, p. 25.

A section of preserved trenches at the Hillman strongpoint. The steps in the foreground lead down to one of the massive bunkers on the site. On the left of the picture is a modern information stand describing the emplacement. *(Author)*

Further to the left St-Aubin-d'Arquenay can be seen, through which the remainder of the battalion passed to attack Rover from the north-east. 185th Brigade's third battalion, 2 Warwicks, had intended to advance on the right of 2 KSLI's column towards Caen, but was switched to the division's left flank to help the hard-pressed airborne troops. The battalion followed 1 Norfolks through St-Aubin-d'Arquenay and then pressed on to Bénouville.

Slightly to the rear of the spot the tour has now reached, on the right in the middle distance, is the reservoir that marks Point 61. On the crest of the hill, just in front and to the right, is Beauvais Farm. This was the furthest point for 1 Suffolks' advance on D-Day. After capturing Hillman, D Company moved up this road and seized the fortified farm buildings just before dark, to consolidate the battalion's forward positions. D Company took the area with little trouble as the German garrison of two officers and 48 men immediately gave themselves up. They had no intention of fighting, for in the courtyard of the farm 1 Suffolks found that the Germans had laid out their packs and belongings in groups of three, ready for their move into captivity when the appropriate moment to surrender had arrived.

DIRECTIONS: Continue along the road to the crest of the ridge, before the dip down a long hill towards Beuville.

THE SITE: From here you have an excellent view to Caen. On the left is a small wood beyond Norfolk House. This was the area in which 1 Norfolks bivouacked on the night of D-Day. From here, the next day, they advanced down the hill and across to Lébisey Wood, 4 km away, to team up with 2 Warwicks in the abortive battle against the men of 21st Panzer Division.

DIRECTIONS: At the bottom of the hill take the left fork along the Avenue du Château. Continue through the next junction in the direction of Blainville (the road is now the D141). Follow the road around to the left and out into open country.

THE SITE: You are now crossing the route that 1 Norfolks took on the move up to Lébisey Wood. In the distance on the right, almost 3 km away, is Lébisey Wood, running along the crest of a line of high ground. 2 Warwicks attacked the ridge from a point to the south-west of Blainville, ahead and to the right.

DIRECTIONS: Follow the D141 into the centre of Blainville-sur-Orne. At the junction, just past the church, you arrive in the village square. Turn to the left, sign-posted to Ouistreham and Caen. At the small roundabout, continue across on the D141.

BATTLEFIELD TOURS

THE SITE: The monument on the right is dedicated to 1 Norfolks, who liberated the village on 7 June, although the first troops to arrive here were actually of 2 Warwicks. They had advanced through St-Aubin-d'Arquenay and cleared the Germans from around Bénouville, before moving south to the northern outskirts of Blainville. Here they anchored 3rd Infantry Division's south-eastern flank late on the evening of D-Day. The next morning 2 Warwicks advanced through the village and formed up to the south to begin their ill-fated attack on Lébisey Wood.

THIS IS THE END OF THE TOUR: Continue on the D141 to the junction. From here you must decide whether you wish to go back to Ouistreham, or perhaps visit Caen.

TOUR F

INLAND, THE WEST FLANK

OBJECTIVE: This tour traces the route of the counter-attack made by GenMaj Feuchtinger's 21st Panzer Division against British 3rd Infantry Division on the late afternoon of 6 June. It is not possible to drive down the axis of the German armoured attack from south to north as all of this was over open ground. The tour visits certain points along the route and is combined with a visit to some of the villages and positions encountered by 9th Infantry Brigade on its move towards Caen.

DURATION/SUITABILITY: The tour covers some 27 km; allow at least 4 hours by car. For the cyclist: the tour uses good quiet roads, but there are lots of small hills. For the disabled: excellent, all major sites accessible by car.

DIRECTIONS: Begin at Field Marshal Montgomery's statue as before. Proceed south along the D60a to Colleville and go in to the centre of the village, past the church and the *mairie* liberated by 1 Suffolks. Go over the crossroads in the centre and look for the sign to Caen on the right. About 100 metres beyond the sign turn right at the almost hidden road junction. Go over the small

Langrune-sur-Mer

Luc-sur-Mer

Douvres-
La-Délivrande

la Délivrande

Lion-sur-Mer

le Haut Lion

le Moulin

la Brèche d'Hermanville

Colleville-
Montgomery-Plage

a

j

Cresserons

Hermanville-
sur-Mer

PÉRIERS

i

Plumetot

WN-16
(MORRIS)

2

Colleville-
Montgomery

RIDGE

POINT 61

1

WN-17
(HILLMAN)

St-Aubin-d'Arquenay

Anisy

c

Mathieu

b

Périers-sur-le-Dan

ROVER

Bénouville

COMMUNE

de Biéville-Beuville

Biéville

Blainville-sur-

e

d

g

Cambes-
en-Plaine

f

h

k

Épron

HÉROUVILLE-
ST-CLAIR

CAEN

① Position of British anti-tank screen

② Position of B Squadron, SY

a Statue of FM Montgomery

b Monument to 3rd Infantry Division

c Canadian monument to
Queen's Own Rifles of Canada

d Monument to 2 RUR

e Cambes-en-Plaine Commonwealth
War Graves Cemetery

f Cambes church

g Monument to 2 KOSB

h Monument to 1 Suffolks

i Reservoir

j Château de Lion-sur-Mer

k Château de la Londe

Base map: IGN 1612OT

0.5   1

Kilometres

crossroads immediately ahead and follow the road (still the D60a) round to the left and out of the village.

THE SITE: You are now going up towards the crossroads at Point 61. Off to the left can be seen the steel cupolas and a few trees which mark the site of Hillman, visited on Tour E. Over on the right but hidden by the curve of the ridge is the road leading southwards from Hermanville, along which the armoured column of 185th Infantry Brigade made its advance to Caen.

DIRECTIONS: This road joins from the right at the crossroads on the top of the hill. Turn left towards Caen. You are now on top of the eastern portion of the strategically important Périers Ridge, seized during the early afternoon of D-Day. Continue across the plateau and then begin down its southern slopes.

THE SITE: As you look southwards across the beautiful countryside towards Caen in the distance, it is easy to see just why British possession of this ridge put the Germans to such a disadvantage. Once 185th Infantry Brigade had placed its long-barrelled 17-pounder Staffordshire Yeomanry Sherman Firefly tanks here and supplemented their firepower with the anti-tank guns of 41st Anti-tank Battery, this force commanded the ground to the south for several kilometres. When 21st Panzer Division counter-attacked straight at these heights with lesser Panzer IVs it was inevitable they would suffer considerable loss.

DIRECTIONS: Continue down the hill to the bottom into the valley carved out by the diminutive River Dan and look for the turning on the right which leads to the village of Périers-sur-le-Dan. Turn right here onto the Périers road (D222) and continue towards the village for a short distance and stop.

THE SITE: You are now on the right flank of 185th Infantry Brigade's push to Caen on D-Day beneath the brigade's supporting anti-tank guns and armour. From this commanding position the brigade was able to engage the tanks of 21st Panzer Division as they came across the ground to the left.

DIRECTIONS: Carry on along the road, past the isolated chapel with a French cemetery surrounding it on the right, and down into the village of Périers-sur-le-Dan. Enter the village via Rue de l'Église along a long straight section of road.

THE SITE: Set back on the left at the end of the road next to the *mairie* is a memorial to 3rd Infantry Division. On the bottom is a brass plaque commemorating those killed in the liberation of the village and who were temporarily buried here: the list of units includes 2 KSLI, 33rd Field Regiment, RA, 1 S Lancs' signals unit and 7th Field Regiment, RA.

Memorial in Périers-sur-le-Dan to the men of British 3rd Infantry Division who died during the liberation of the area. *(Author)*

DIRECTIONS: Continue through the village to the give-way sign at the junction with the D220. Carry on across the junction to join the D220 towards Mathieu. Leave Périers and continue across open ground with Caen away to the left.

THE SITE: On the right is a small area of woodland about 1.5 km away across open fields, with the village of Plumetot just beyond. The tanks of 100th/22nd Panzer Regiment and some half-tracks of 192nd Panzergrenadier Regiment crossed the road in this vicinity from south to north on their drive to the sea on D-Day. Their start line near Lébisey Wood can be seen in the far left distance, to the left of the prominent water tower on the horizon. The German tanks that passed through here were sheltered by Périers village from the worst of the fire from British 3rd Infantry Division. They continued to the north-west towards

Plumetot only to come under more fire from guns sited near Point 61 as they climbed up the western edge of Périers Ridge.

DIRECTIONS: Drive into the village of Mathieu to the road junction, then turn right towards Caen along the D141.

THE SITE: 2 KOSB captured Mathieu without a fight on 7 June as the battalion advanced from its assembly area near Hermanville towards Cambes-en-Plaine. This spared the village great damage initially, but Mathieu was later used as a rear area during the four weeks of stalemate in this sector following the landings and was bombarded sporadically by German artillery.

DIRECTIONS: Continue past the church on the left to the crossroads and take the left-hand turning on the D220 towards Anisy, past more fine walled buildings and courtyards. The road twists and turns, crossing a small roundabout, but continue to follow the D220 out of the village and over the bridge across the dual carriageway from Douvres to Caen, to a roundabout. Take the second exit from the roundabout towards Anisy.

THE SITE: This gap of countryside between Mathieu and Anisy was another route that 192nd Panzergrenadier Regiment took on its counter-attack. The units of the regiment that assembled near Cambes to the south formed the left flank of GenMaj Feuchtinger's counter-attack against 3rd Infantry Division. They continued northwards across the area near the roundabout, then swung north-eastwards to pass west of Cresserons into the gap separating Canadian 3rd Infantry Division and British 3rd Infantry Division, and made it to the sea.

DIRECTIONS: Continue towards Anisy. After about 200 metres on the right there is a memorial to the Queen's Own Rifles of Canada, who took Anisy on 6 June. The tour has now strayed onto the ground that led inland from the landings on Juno Beach. Go on 200 metres and take the turning to the left towards Cambes-en-Plaine (D220a). Leave Anisy and begin to pass across open fields towards Cambes. Pull over and stop where safe.

THE SITE: On the left ahead is the small hamlet of le Mesnil surrounded by trees. Cambes is directly ahead. In the early

A Panzer IV of 12th SS Panzer Division moving through a French village towards the landings. The Germans had to move carefully to avoid the attention of Allied fighter-bombers. Their convoys were well spaced out and took a great length of time to complete any move. *(Bundesarchiv 1011/493/3355/10)*

afternoon of 7 June, 1 KOSB arrived in le Mesnil and was subjected to concentrated German fire, later being joined by 2 RUR. Later that afternoon 2 RUR launched a company-strength attack on Cambes, supported by a squadron of East Riding Yeomanry tanks, along the small track that links le Mesnil and Cambes. The attackers engaged 1st Battalion, 25th SS Panzergrenadier Regiment, from 12th SS Panzer Division *Hitlerjugend* in the village, and broke off with considerable loss.

A second, much larger, attempt by 2 RUR took place two days later. From the direction of Anisy, the whole battalion advanced on Cambes across the open ground to the right and left. The D220a road on which the tour is now travelling formed the axis of the attack. 2 RUR got into the wood on this northern side of Cambes, but met with stiff opposition. Late in the day 1 KOSB joined 2 RUR and the wood and the village were cleared.

SS-Unterscharführer (Corporal) Helmut Stöcker, 1st Infantry Gun Company, 12th SS Panzer Division, was in Cambes on 7 June.

'We reached Cambes and drove into a small ravine. Suddenly, there was the sound of tracks in the village.

Some 50 metres in front of us a Sherman came out of a side road. It stopped in the intersection and spotted us and our guns. The turret of the tank immediately swung towards us and before we knew what was happening, the first shell was fired. We saved ourselves by jumping to the left over a locked gate. Some of the crews were still by the guns when the first shell slammed through the tractors and guns. We were fortunate since it was an anti-tank shell which kept on going. If it had been an explosive shell, we would have had it. A few moments later, an infantryman from I Battalion knocked the Sherman out with his Panzerfaust.'

Source: Hubert Meyer, *The History of the 12. SS Panzerdivision 'Hitlerjugend'*, p. 44.

For the next four weeks Cambes was the right-hand position of 3rd Infantry Division's lodgement and received continual bombardment from the guns of 12th SS and 21st Panzer Divisions. The battlefield resembled those of the worst days of the First World War, with both sides dug in just a few hundred metres apart and watching every movement. Things did not change until Montgomery reorganised the Allied line prior to his big offensive against Caen, Operation 'Charnwood', on 8 July. British 59th Infantry Division had by then moved into this sector of the line and launched its attack from the area of Cambes. British 3rd Infantry Division was also part of this operation and attacked Lébisey in strength, while Canadian 3rd Infantry Division advanced towards Carpiquet. By 10 July, British troops were in the northern part of Caen, but still well short of their D-Day objective.

DIRECTIONS: Continue along the road to the edge of Cambes. At the entrance to Cambes is a road junction where the track from le Mesnil joins from the left. Turn right and park.

THE SITE: This is the northern edge of the village, with its centre and church about 500 metres to the south. In 1944, this part of the village contained a small wood surrounded by a high stone wall which caused all manner of problems to the attacking infantry and their supporting armour. On the left of the road by the corner is a memorial commemorating 2 RUR's capture of the

Commonwealth War Graves Cemetery at Cambes, located inside the walled wood at the edge of the village. This area was part of the static front line for four weeks following the landings. *(Author)*

village on 9 June. A few metres down the road, also on the left, is the Cambes-en-Plaine Commonwealth War Graves Cemetery. There are 223 known burials here with just one unknown soldier. Many of the fallen are from the South and North Staffordshire Regiments, who died in the area during the battle to take Caen on 8 and 9 July.

DIRECTIONS: Return to your car and continue past the cemetery. The road bears round to the left in a wide sweep. Continue past the church and then turn left. Stop in the square by the *mairie* opposite the church.

THE SITE: On one side of the road is a big stone plinth in remembrance of the French civilians who were killed during the fighting. On the opposite side is another memorial to the liberators, both of 59th (Staffordshire) Infantry Division and of 3rd Infantry Division. A small stone tablet bolted on to the monument is dedicated to 2 RUR. This part of the village was the scene of severe fighting during 9 June, when 2 RUR captured Cambes from 12th SS Panzer Division.

DIRECTIONS: From the memorials carry on round to the left and continue towards the end of the road and a T-junction. After about 200 metres you pass through the remains of Cambes Wood.

THE SITE: In 1944, this area was crossed by trenches and dug-outs and defended by infantry backed by tanks. It was in this section of the line that 9th Infantry Brigade's three battalions had to endure weeks of holding the front, shelled and mortared all the while by the enemy just a few hundred metres away to the south.

The remains of the high stone wall which once surrounded the wood at Cambes. In the left centre of the picture is a memorial to 1 KOSB of 9th Infantry Brigade, who held the front line here for almost a month. *(Author)*

DIRECTIONS: At the road junction turn right and continue back past the cemetery. Turn right onto the D220a again along Rue de Lt Lynn, dedicated to an officer who was killed in the fighting on 8 July 1944.

THE SITE: Near here on 13 June the commander of British 3rd Infantry Division, Maj-Gen Rennie, was wounded when his carrier hit a mine. He was replaced by Maj-Gen Whistler, who commanded 3rd Infantry Division until the end of the war. Rennie recovered from his injuries and took command of 51st (Highland) Division. He was killed in March 1945.

DIRECTIONS: Continue a short distance along the road and look to the right into the remains of Cambes Wood alongside the war cemetery.

THE SITE: A commemorative plaque on a section of stone wall can be seen after about 50 metres. This is a memorial to the men of 1 KOSB who fought and died in the wood. Alongside is a section of the old stone wall which surrounded the wood. More evidence of the structure can be seen amongst the trees on the right as you proceed along the road. Ahead, just over 500 metres away, is the hamlet of la Bijude and the site of lines defended by 21st Panzer Division while 9th Infantry Brigade held Cambes. In the month following this first clash, the Germans turned la Bijude into a fortress criss-crossed with deep trenches and weapons pits and fronted by a deep anti-tank ditch. The road the tour is travelling down follows close to the route of the old railway line from Caen to Luc-sur-Mer, which marked the divisional boundary between 21st and 12th SS Panzer Divisions.

DIRECTIONS: At the end of the road turn left onto the D79b, signposted to Caen. On the right is wide-open country looking across to the village of Mâlon and the city of Caen.

THE SITE: This ground was not captured by Allied forces until more than four weeks after D-Day. As you approach la Bijude, if you look slightly to the rear and away to the right, the buildings of the hamlet of Galmanche can be seen. This was the right-hand position of 12th SS Panzer Division during the fighting in Cambes.

Some 3 km away to the south is the area of la Folie. It was there that GenLt Richter had his command bunker during the battle. This is now incorporated into the Mémorial de Caen.

> *Generalleutnant* **Wilhelm Richter, commander of 716th Infantry Division, recalls conditions in Normandy.**
>
> 'The division commander of the SS-Div "Hitlerjugend" arrived and was briefed by me. He said to me almost verbally [sic], "I have been on my way to you for about eight hours; more than four hours I spent in road ditches because of air attacks. The march columns of the division are suffering bad losses in manpower and material." The commander of the Panzer Lehr Division liaison detachment had expressed the same view a short time before. The Panzer Lehr Division had to be supplied with gasoline by my division so that it could move up its tanks,

Then: Château de la Londe, during the battle to enlarge the lodgement in late June. The building has been reduced to a shell by artillery fire from the German lines just a few hundred metres away at la Bijude. *(IWM B6217)*

Now: The rebuilt Château de la Londe, which was wrecked in the struggle to reach Caen. The area around the château was the scene of some of the most intense close-quarters fighting endured by British 3rd Infantry Division. *(Author)*

since its own gasoline supply column had been set on fire for the most part by enemy air attacks. Therefore the tanks did not arrive until 7th June after many hours delay.'

Source: Post-war interview, US National Archives, B-621.

DIRECTIONS: At the roundabout take the third exit signposted to Périers-sur-le-Dan. Drive round to the right and then on the right is the beautifully proportioned Château de la Londe set back along a tree-lined drive. Pull into the side of the road just after the gates of the drive and stop by the memorial.

THE SITE: The memorial is dedicated to 1 Suffolks, who finally captured the château at the end of June. Alongside is a plinth bearing a very good map and description of 1 Suffolks' final attacks. Next, after 300 metres, is the walled farm of la Londe and then another 200 metres further on is le Londel, set back amidst a wooded area. These three locations were the scene of much heavy fighting by 8th Infantry Brigade in the weeks following the invasion. The area earned the nickname of 'the bloodiest square mile in Normandy'.

DIRECTIONS: Carry on towards Périers. Go across the small crossroads and stop about 200 metres short of the village.

THE SITE: There is open farmland on either side of the road over which Colonel von Oppeln attacked with his panzers on D-Day. Ahead and beyond the village can be seen the Périers Ridge running across the skyline. The villages of Beuville and Biéville can be seen behind and to the right. Lébisey Wood, the starting point for Oppeln's counter-attack, can be seen behind in the far distance. The gaps through which the panzers attempted to drive on either side of the village can also be clearly discerned.

DIRECTIONS: Carry straight on down into Périers village to a T-junction. Turn left and then take the next right, signposted Colleville. Take the next road left (D222) after 100 metres towards Plumetot.

THE SITE: The tour is now climbing the Périers Ridge with the ground still rising on the right. On moving up to the crest the

BATTLEFIELD TOURS

ground opens out on either side to give good views to the north and south. The panzers came through on the left and were caught by more British guns firing from behind and to the right near Point 61. At the top of the rising ground look away to the right; the coast is clearly visible. This is the area where Lieutenant Rudolf Schaaf had his mobile 155-mm guns of 10th Battery, 1716th Artillery Regiment, firing onto Sword Beach.

DIRECTIONS: Continue along the top of the ridge to where the road begins to drop down towards Plumetot. Stop just before the reservoir buried in a green mound.

THE SITE: From here there is a panoramic view of the western side of British 3rd Infantry Division's beachhead. The ground between Lion-sur-Mer and Luc-sur-Mer is clearly visible ahead and to the right. Across to the right in the middle distance is a prominent cream-coloured barn. To the left of this barn is the ground through which the panzergrenadiers and a few tanks of 21st Panzer Division passed to arrive on the coast on the evening of D-Day. The wood in the far distance is in the grounds of the château at Lion.

DIRECTIONS: Continue down the hill into Plumetot. Plumetot was taken without a fight on 7 June. Pass round alongside and behind the church on the D222 towards Cresserons. Turn right at the junction there onto the D221 and proceed through the village then turn right at the next junction and then again almost immediately turn left, continuing along the D221, signposted Lion-sur-Mer, and out into open country.

Further along to the right the lower slopes of Périers Ridge sweep down to Lion-sur-Mer. It was over this ground that Schaaf led his guns against 41 RM Commando, forcing the British to retreat into positions around the church in the town.

Continue down the long straight to arrive at the wall round the grounds of the château of Lion-sur-Mer on the left. Go straight on at the traffic lights and continue to the roundabout on the western limits of Lion-sur-Mer close by the sea.

THIS IS THE END OF THE TOUR: Turn right at the first exit on the roundabout and drive eastwards towards Ouistreham to return to Monty's statue.

PART FOUR

ON YOUR
RETURN

FURTHER RESEARCH

If you have undertaken the battlefield tours included in this book and are intrigued to know more about the landings on Sword Beach, there are several places to visit in England and books to read which will give you a fuller understanding of the action.

Some of the troops who landed on Sword Beach on D-Day left from Portsmouth. There is now an excellent museum dedicated to the Normandy landings along the seafront from Portsmouth Dockyard at Southsea. The **D-Day Museum** is open throughout the year and has an interesting range of items on display including a modern version of the Bayeux Tapestry in reverse; the D-Day Tapestry depicts the 20th century invasion from England to Normandy.

The **Imperial War Museum** in London is also another good source of information and exhibits relating to the invasion. The museum also holds the photographic archive of all official war pictures, including cine film. The photographic reference room can be visited by appointment to view these or to buy prints from the archive. Pictures can also be ordered by post if you know the appropriate negative number. The photographs used in this book are just samples of the thousands of pictures the museum holds relating to the fighting in Normandy.

Eisenhower's advanced headquarters before the invasion was located at Southwick House north of Portsmouth. It was at Southwick House that the final decision to launch the invasion was made. This was also the location of the headquarters of the naval component of the invasion, Operation Neptune. The original wall chart showing the naval position of the landings at H-Hour on 6 June 1944 is still displayed. The house is now part of the naval base of HMS *Dryad* and as such is closed to the public. However, during the 50th anniversary of D-Day in 1994, Southwick House was open to the public on specific days for a short period. This may well happen again during the 60th anniversary in 2004.

The internet is another good source of information regarding

Above: Memorial at the junction of Queen and Roger sectors of Sword Beach to the commandos who landed nearby. *(Author)*

Page 185: Commandos of Brigadier Lord Lovat's 1st Special Service Brigade moving inland. They have just left the beach and are heading for Colleville, making a detour to the right to avoid a minefield. *(IWM B5063)*

the landings, although most of the easily accessible material tends to be lightweight and general rather than specific and detailed. Two good sites are <www.dday.co.uk> and <www.ddaymuseum.co.uk>. New sites are being added all the time, so the best option is to go onto a friendly search engine – <www.google.co.uk> for instance – and type in D-Day. Also worth pursuing are the sites devoted to individual regiments involved in the landings. Simply type in the name of the regiment on a search engine and browse through the findings.

For those students of the war who wish to delve deeper into official publications and archives to examine highly detailed reports of the landings the following might be useful. The Imperial War Museum has copies of all of the official histories of the units and battalions that were engaged in the action and these can be consulted in its reading room by appointment. The National Archives (formerly the Public Record Office) at Kew in London holds the war diaries of all of the units that served in Normandy. This archive also has unpublished after-action reports and summaries of the various battles. Access to this material can be had a few minutes after applying for a reader's ticket.

A more accessible and broader view of the landings can be gained from the wide range of books published on the invasion.

Included here is a select bibliography of some that might be useful:

Anon., *Operation 'Neptune' Landings in Normandy, June 1944*, HMSO, London, 1994.

Anon., *Royal Engineers Battlefield Tour: Normandy to the Seine*, BAOR.

Anon, *The Story of the 79th Armoured Division*, Privately published, 1946.

Blandford, Edmund, *Two Sides of the Beach*, Airlife, Shrewsbury, 1999.

Carell, Paul, *Invasion – They're Coming!*, George Harrap, London, 1962.

Chazette, Alain, *Le Mur de l'Atlantique en Normandie*, Heimdal, Bayeux, 2000.

D'Este, Carlo, *Decision in Normandy*, Collins, London, 1983.

Ellis, L.F., *Victory In The West*, HMSO, London, 1962.

Ford, Ken, *D-Day 1944: Sword Beach & the British Airborne Landings*, Osprey, Oxford, 2002.

Hastings, Max, *Overlord*, Michael Joseph, London, 1984.

Isby, David C., (ed.), *Fighting The Invasion: The German Army at D-Day*, Greenhill Books, London, 2000.

Lincoln, John, *Thank God and the Infantry*, Alan Sutton, Stroud, 1994.

Lovat, Lord, *March Past*, Weidenfeld & Nicolson, London, 1978.

Luck, Hans von, *Panzer Commander*, Cassell, London, 1989.

McDougall, Murdoch, *Swiftly They Struck*, Odhams, London, 1954.

Meyer, Hubert, *The History of the 12. SS Panzerdivision 'Hitlerjugend'*, J.J. Fedorowicz, Winnipeg, Canada, 1994.

Neillands, Robin, & de Normann, Roderick, *D-Day 1944*, Orion, London, 1994.

Radcliffe, G.L.Y., *The King's Shropshire Light Infantry*, Blackwell, Oxford, 1957.

Ramsey, Winston G., (ed.), *D-Day Then and Now*, Battle of Britain Prints International, London, 1995.

Saunders, Hilary St George, *The Green Beret*, Michael Joseph, London, 1949.

Scarfe, Norman, *Assault Division*, Collins, London, 1947.

Tute, Warren; Costello, John; & Hughes, Terry; *D-Day*, Sidgwick & Jackson, London, 1974.

Underhill, D.F., *The Queen's Own Royal Staffordshire Yeomanry*, Staffordshire Libraries, Stafford, 1994.

INDEX

Page numbers in *italics* denote an illustration.